THE
LITTLE
BOOK
OF
BASIC
STYLE

THE
LITTLE
BOOK
OF
BASIC
STYLE

How to Write a Program
You Can Read

JOHN M. NEVISON

John M. Nevison Associates
Boston, Massachusetts

Illustrations by
Victoria Cowling Chu

ADDISON-WESLEY PUBLISHING COMPANY
Reading, Massachusetts · Menlo Park, California
London · Amsterdam · Don Mills, Ontario · Sydney

This book is in the
ADDISON-WESLEY SERIES IN JOY OF COMPUTING

The language BASIC was developed at Dartmouth College by John G. Kemeny and Thomas E. Kurtz.

This book was reproduced by Addison-Wesley from camera-ready proof supplied by the author. The book was designed by Nancy Ross McJennett, set in Palatino, and composed using programs developed by Stephen V. F. Waite at Dartmouth College. The text was prepared on the Dartmouth Time-Sharing System and supplied to a typesetting machine at Imperial Company, Hartford, Vermont.

Figure 1.1 is from G. Polya, How to Solve It: A New Aspect of Mathematical Method *(copyright 1945 © 1973 by Princeton University Press; Princeton Paperback, 1971), pp.xvi-xvii. Reprinted by permission of Princeton University Press.*

Second printing, August 1978

ISBN 0-201-05247-4
DEFGHIJKL-AL-8987654321

Contents

4 CODE: THE NAKED FORM   51

5 EXAMPLES: THE PROGRAM AT WORK AND PLAY   89

6 BEYOND BASIC: LARGER PROGRAMS   115

Preface

This book is for anyone who wishes to write better Basic programs, from junior high student to research scientist to corporate executive to home computer freak. William Strunk once wrote a book on how to write clear English. E. B. White revised the book and saw it republished as *The Elements of Style*. White says that Strunk, taking pride in the original's brevity, referred to it as "the little book." This book takes its title from that phrase.

The volume is slim but, I hope, substantial. Each rule was written to be read and reread. You can quickly read the book cover to cover, but if you try and follow its rules, you will find occasion to refer to them from time to time.

Why Rules of Style?

You may well ask "Why follow any rules?" The answer is quite simple: because they will help you write a better program. A better program is one that is more likely to be correct, one that is easier to read, and one that is simple to use. For a number of years flow charts have been advocated as a way to help explain programs, but now there is evidence that they do not help (Shneiderman, 1977). On the other hand, style does help. It puts the structure where it should be: in the program itself.

A deeper reason for using these rules of style is that they offer an approach to structured programming. If you look closely, you can see how a person accustomed to writing a well-styled Basic program can move on to writing well-structured programs in other languages. Basic can not honestly be called a structured language, but a well-styled program can begin the move toward structure.

The rules leave the writer wide latitude for building a program. The illustrative examples show the author's favorite solution to a stylistic problem, but not the only solution. For example, while indentation is absolutely necessary, the size of the indentation is very much a matter of individual preference. Another example is the REM-5 convention to distinguish comment from code. The convention is merely one convenient solution, but the rule is unequivocal: comment must be distinguished from code.

Novice Reader, Expert Reader

Anyone who has written and run a computer program is *literate* in computing. To become *fluent*, however, takes time and practice. Rules of style can reduce the time and practice necessary to turn out a truly legible, correct program. They offer a way to think about the program that encourages thoughtful organization.

No one easily yields a pet programming practice and anyone who has written a dozen programs will find several rules in this book annoying. Some rules may appear tedious to follow, for example, the rules about typing. Some may conflict with an experienced programmer's idea of good style. A few may seem too obvious to bear mention. The person who cares enough about a program's style to argue with these rules probably has little need of them. On the other hand, an argument against any rule should be advanced for the same reason the rule itself was suggested: because there is a better way to make the program read.

Thoughtful use of blank lines and indentation is a central theme of this book. It dramatically increases the legibility of a program, but requires attentive typing. The seasoned, but sloppy, programmer can avoid much tedium by writing a program that will automatically format his or her unkempt programs according to rules 3, 16, 17, and 18. One such program is included in Chapter 6.

Standard Basic

A word about standard Basic. The American National Standards Institute has defined an ANSI Basic to take its place beside ANSI Fortran and ANSI Cobol. The defined Basic is called Minimal Basic. It is a small kernel of Basic from which future extensions such as plotting and string manipulation will grow. The proposed standard makes one severe mistake: it does not require a program to accept a simple blank line. Many smart implementations allow this convenience; many stupid implementations do not. The REM-5 convention in Rule 3 allows anyone to write a legible, pseudo-blank line in Minimal Basic. By using the REM-5 convention, every example in this book may be expressed in standard Basic.

Some implementations of Basic insist on justifying every statement to the left. Such justification has no justification. It destroys any system of indentation and reduces a legible program to a column of statements. This particularly malicious habit may be forestalled, if not eliminated, with a formatting tool like the program in Chapter 6.

The One-Page Program

This book limits itself to Basic programs *less than one page long*. Building a much larger program strains several features of the language, most notably its control structures. If you plan to write a large program you should learn something about structured programming and learn a language that allows you to write structured programs easily. Such languages include Dartmouth's Structured Basic, PL/1, Cobol, or Algol. One of the fundamental tenets of structured programming is that each unit of a program should be no longer than one page. Learning to write small Basic programs can be an excellent introduction to writing these elementary units.

Chapter 6 contains a few suggestions for the truant spirit who aspires to write a large program in Basic. These suggestions are included because some readers will have no structured language available, only Basic.

Acknowledgments

The easy-to-use Dartmouth Time-Sharing System, both the one at CallData and the one at Dartmouth, ran the programs in this book. The text was set on the Dartmouth system. Both systems speeded the writing of the book.

I would like to acknowledge the special help of Stephen Garland at Dartmouth. Many of the book's strengths are the result of his careful criticism. I would also like to thank Timothy Stein for proofreading STYLIST, Stephen Waite for his help with the computerized typesetting, Nancy Farrell and Linda Micheli for their meticulous proofreading, William Gruener for being an editor who takes an enthusiastic interest in his books, and Nancy Ross McJennett for her dual performance as critical professional designer and tolerant wife. The many errors that remain are, regrettably, the fault of the author.

John M. Nevison
Boston, 1977

FROM
PROBLEM
SOLVING
TO
PROGRAM
WRITING

1

He who has nothing to assert has no style and can have none.

GEORGE BERNARD SHAW
Man and Superman

Early in the development of Western languages the Greeks wrote boustrophedon, the way the ox plows, with lines reading back and forth down the page. Boustrophedon was efficient for the eye but not for the reader: it required two kinds of reading, forward and backward. The system was simplified to make every line read left to right. Later the Greeks began to notch the long column of text with an occasional indented line to give the eye a place to rest. The paragraph was born. Since that time many conventions have evolved to ease communication between writer and reader.

Computer languages, however, are still in their infancy, and much remains to be learned about how to improve communication between the writer and the reader of a computer program. The language Basic is now only thirteen years old. It is simple to learn and quick to write, but whether or not it is easy to read depends heavily on how it is written. While some Basic programs read like unnotched boustrophedon, others read quickly and clearly. The purpose of this book is to help the writer prepare a program that is correct and *easy to read*.

Even the hermit programmer who never shows a line of code to another human being knows that a program must not only run successfully, it must *read* successfully. For even the hermit must read his own programs, and because he is as fallible as the rest of us, he will read his program several times before he removes all of his errors. If he writes programs that are easy to read, he will save himself time.

In addition to helping the hermit in all of us, the rules in this book can have a dramatic effect when we emerge from our caves to show off our working programs: we will be able to understand each other. Among the many programs we write a few may impress everyone with their clarity. Perhaps we will say these programs have style.

5

Problem Solving

Anyone involved in writing a computer program is involved in solving a variety of problems, from how to make the computer do something useful to how to make the program easy for someone to use. A programmer probably does grow better at solving problems because of experience in writing computer programs, but why this should be so is imperfectly understood. One reason for this limited understanding is that problem solving itself remains largely a mystery.

A few tentative ideas on how this process works are available today. Mathematics offers a collection of problems that are free of most of the distractions that obscure real problems. George Polya has used mathematics as a laboratory for exploring problem solving. In his book, *How To Solve It*, he suggests a general approach to a problem: understand the problem, devise a plan to solve it, carry out the plan, and review the solution. When you begin to explore a problem that may be solved with a computer, you can learn much from Polya's systematic approach.

As Figure 1.1 suggests, part of understanding the problem is understanding what the problem is *not*. A programmer should always ask first whether the problem needs a computer to solve it. When you are interested in results, sometimes they may be achieved faster and easier in another way. Several of the programs in this book, for example, can be worked on certain pocket calculators. A jumble of ninety names can be quickly sorted by writing them on three-by-five cards and arranging the cards.

After understanding the problem and being convinced that it should be solved with a computer program, you develop a plan to solve it. Even after a plan has been worked out you should continue to search for alternatives. Frequently a better plan will emerge. The search for a better alternative may succeed just as the first plan has been carried out. Do not be afraid to start over if the improvement merits the extra work.

Accomplishing the Work and Composing the Program

The subject of this book, how to write a program you can read, is itself one step in composing a computer program that in turn is one step in getting work done on a computer. Figure 1.2 decomposes the solutions to these two problems into their constituent elements. The most important lesson of Figure 1.2 is that a computer program has a larger purpose than the beauty of its function: it must help someone do useful work. Understanding this real work and what portion of it will be solved with computing is the programmer's first and most important task.

Understanding the Problem

What is the unknown? What are the data? What is the condition? Is it possible to satisfy the condition? Is the condition sufficient to determine the unknown? Or is it insufficient? Or redundant? Or contradictory? Draw a figure. Introduce suitable notation. Separate the various parts of the condition. Can you write them down?

Devising a Plan

Have you seen it before? Or have you seen the same problem in a slightly different form? Do you know a related problem? Do you know a theorem that could be useful? Look at the unknown! And try to think of a familiar problem having the same or a similar unknown.

Here is a problem related to yours and solved before. Could you use it? Could you use its result? Could you use its method? Should you introduce some auxiliary element in order to make its use possible? Could you restate the problem? Could you restate it still differently? Go back to definitions.

If you cannot solve the proposed problem try to solve first some related problem. Could you imagine a more accessible related problem? A more general problem? A more special problem? An analogous problem? Could you solve a part of the problem? Keep only a part of the condition, drop the other part; how far is the unknown then determined, how can it vary? Could you derive something useful from the data? Could you think of other data appropriate to determine the unknown? Could you change the unknown or the data, or both if necessary, so that the new unknown and the new data are nearer to each other? Did you use all the data? Did you use the whole condition? Have you taken into account all essential notions involved in the problem?

Carrying Out the Plan

Carrying out your plan of the solution, check each step. Can you see clearly that the step is correct? Can you prove that it is correct?

Examining the Solution

Can you check the result? Can you check the argument? Can you derive the result differently? Can you see it a a glance? Can you use the result, or the method, for some other problem?

Figure 1.1 *Solving a Problem*

The programmer's second task is to beware constantly of how the work will evolve over time to meet changing requirements. Whatever the solution, it will not last forever. Eventually change will render both organization and program obsolete. Beginning with this knowledge can forestall many problems.

Problem	To get work done on a computer	To compose a computer program
Understand the problem.	Know what work is required. (And how it might change over time.)	Know what the program should accomplish.
Devise a plan to solve it.	Organize people and computer programs to accomplish the work. (The organization should be flexible enough to evolve with changing work.)	Design the program. Order the pieces. Select data structure, algorithm, computer, and language. Prepare the test.
Carry out the plan.	Set the organization to work. (Modify the organization as the work changes.)	**Write the program.**
Review the solution.	Review the work to be sure it remains useful. (When the organization becomes obsolete, begin again.)	Test the program.

Figure 1.2   *Accomplish the Work and Compose the Program*

Nested Problems and Top-Down Solutions

Figure 1.2 is outlined in Figure 1.3 to show how solving the first problem gave birth to the second. During the struggle to understand the original problem, or to devise the plan, or to carry out the plan, many subproblems can occur. Each of these subproblems may be solved with the same four-step process. A tough problem may spawn a host of minor problems and the problem solver may get quite confused while dealing with them all. A great aid to working out the solution to a family of problems is to keep them in their place by keeping them *nested*.

In Figure 1.3, for example, you must first know what work is required before organizing people and computer programs to accomplish the work. Nesting problems allows you to sort out various levels of the problem. When working on the solution you complete all four steps at one level while

To get work done on a computer.
  I.   Know what work is required
  II. Organize
         A. Computer programs
             To compose a computer program.
             1. Know the program's goal
             2. Design the program
             3. **Write the program**

                 To write a computer program.
                 a. Comment
                 b. Code
                 c. Type
                 d. Practice

             4. Test the program
         B. People
  III. Set the organization to work
  IV. Review the work

Figure 1.3 *Nested Problems*

pretending the subproblems have been solved, go back to the beginning and solve the first level of subproblems—all four steps for each of them— and go back a third time to solve the sub-subproblems, and so on. This approach is known as a top-down solution. It is the rule of the artist who works from the general to the particular. Compose, design, write, test; comment, code, type, practice; *think* top-down.

Benefits of a Well-Written Program

The benefits of a well-written program follow naturally from its position in Figure 1.3. First, it will reduce the time it takes to practice and test. Second, it will be easy to use so it will fit smoothly into the organization of people for whom it must work. Third, it can quickly and accurately be modified to meet changing needs. Fourth, parts of it can frequently be salvaged for use in later programs.

A badly written program will have the opposite effect. It will be slow to test, hard to use, and difficult to modify. Its users will tolerate it only grudgingly and discard it with glee at the first opportunity.

The Distance Between Two Points

To try out this problem solving procedure, try to compose a program to find the distance between two points. To understand the problem, begin by putting the points on a grid. The distance between the points is the shortest distance, that is, a straight line. The grid illustrated in Figure 1.4 is sometimes called a Cartesian coordinate system after its discoverer, Rene Descartes. Call the two points One and Two and put them on the coordinate system pictured in Figure 1.4: One lies at (2,1) and Two at (6,4). The problem is to write a program that will begin with the coordinates of the two points and compute the distance between them.

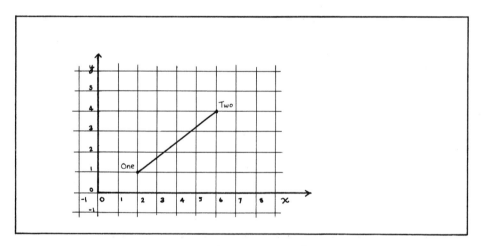

Figure 1.4 *Cartesian Coordinates*

Devising a plan to solve this problem can take some time. The Greek mathematician Pythagoras provided a useful idea. He found that in a right triangle the sum of the squares of the sides is equal to the square of the hypotenuse, or in mathematical terms, $S1 \cdot S1 + S2 \cdot S2 = H \cdot H$, where $S1$ is the first side, $S2$ the second side, and H the hypotenuse.

Pythagoras' hypotenuse can also be the distance between the two points in the problem. So if $S1$ and $S2$ can be found from the coordinates of the two points, the distance between the points can be computed. Descartes knew of Pythagoras' idea and showed that the third point on the grid has coordinates related to the first two.

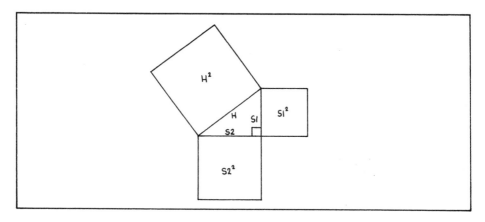

Figure 1.5 *Pythagoras' Idea*

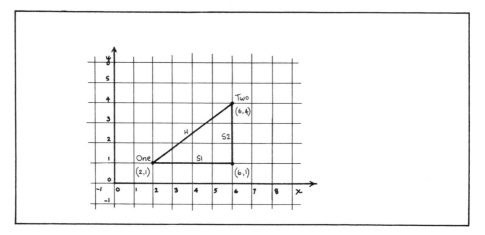

Figure 1.6 *Triangle on Cartesian Coordinates*

With the third point, the two sides can be found and the answer can be calculated. The distance between the original two points turns out to be 5 units. These ideas together suggest how to code the procedure, or algorithm, for the computer program. The data structure is a Cartesian coordinate plane on which two points are located with coordinates.

Data Structure

Notice how the idea of a grid and some sketches and diagrams helped solve the problem. The appropriate data structure often aids the solution. Consider for a moment the structures in Figures 1.7 through 1.12. Each of these ideas can help a computer programmer. When composing a computer program, explore different structures before picking out one to use.

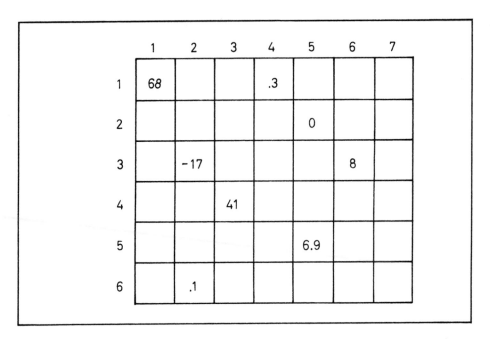

Figure 1.7 *A Table*

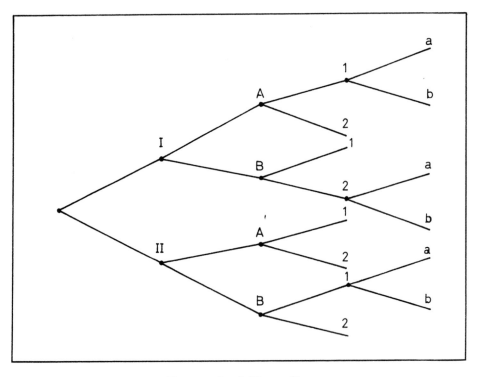

Figure 1.8 *A Binary Tree*

12

Line Number	Next Line Number	DATA	Previous Line Number
1	3		0
2			
3	5		1
4			
5	6		3
6	9		5
7			
8			
9	10		6
10	11		9
11	43		10

Figure 1.9 *A Linked List*

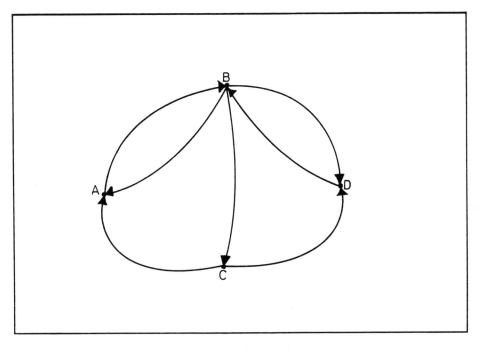

Figure 1.10 *A Directed Graph*

13

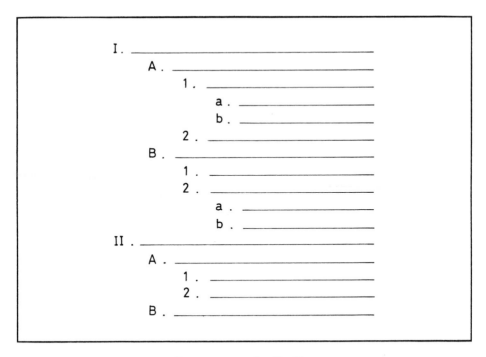

Figure 1.11 *An Outline*

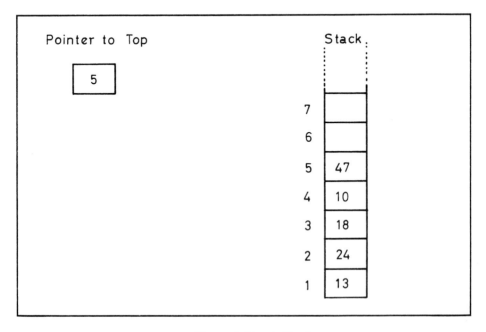

Figure 1.12 *A Stack*

The Proper Algorithm

The word algorithm comes from the surname of the Persian mathematician Abu Ja'far Mohammed ibn Musa al-Khowarizmi. It is a procedure that has been defined so well that a machine can follow it. Designing the algorithm is very close to writing the actual program. Descartes adopted a plan for pursuing his philosophical inquiry that can serve as a guide to designing an algorithm today.

- The first of these was to accept nothing as true which I did not clearly recognise to be so: that is to say, carefully to avoid precipitation and prejudice in judgments, and to accept in them nothing more than what was presented to my mind so clearly and distinctly that I could have no occasion to doubt it.
- The second was to divide up each of the difficulties which I examined into as many parts as possible, and as seemed requisite in order that it might be resolved in the best manner possible.
- The third was to carry on my reflections in due order, commencing with objects that were the most simple and easy to understand, in order to rise little by little, or by degrees, to knowledge of the most complex, assuming an order, even if a fictitious one, among those which do not follow a natural sequence relatively to one another.
- The last was in all cases to make enumerations so complete and reviews so general that I should be certain of having omitted nothing.

Notice how similar Descartes' plan is to Polya's rules. Descartes' plan is a good guide because of his emphasis on ordered parts. A possible algorithm for the distance between two points is:

A. [Input.] Read in the coordinates of the two points, X1,Y1 and X2,Y2.
B. [Computation.] Compute the two sides S1=(X2-X1), S2=(Y2-Y1). Calculate the hypotenuse $H = \sqrt{S1 \cdot S1 + S2 \cdot S2}$.
C. [Output.] Print the number of the trial, the coordinates of the two points, and the distance between them, and quit.

Writing the Program

To pursue the top-down organization of this chapter, assume that the program has already been written and that it looks like this:

```
100 REM      DISTANCE         17 JULY 1977      JOHN M. NEVISON
110
120 REM      FIND THE DISTANCE BETWEEN TWO POINTS, ONE AND
130 REM      TWO.  THE POINTS LIE IN A CARTESIAN
135 REM      COORDINATE SYSTEM.  THE ALGORITHM IS
140 REM      DERIVED FROM THE PYTHAGOREAN THEOREM.
150
160 REM      VARIABLES:
170 REM          H.......THE HYPOTENUSE OF THE TRIANGLE
180 REM                  AND DISTANCE BETWEEN THE POINTS
190 REM          X1,Y1..COORDINATES OF THE FIRST POINT
200 REM          X2,Y2..COORDINATES OF THE SECOND POINT
210 REM          S1,S2..TWO SIDES OF A RIGHT TRIANGLE
220
230 REM      MAIN PROGRAM
240
250          READ X1,Y1,     X2,Y2
255          DATA  2, 1,      6, 4
260
270          LET S1 = X2 - X1
280          LET S2 = Y2 - Y1
290          LET H = SQR(S1*S1 + S2*S2)
300
310          PRINT X1;Y1,    X2;Y2,      H
320
330          END
```

When the program runs it prints the following results:

```
2   1           6   4           5
```

Reviewing the Solution

After the program runs, it should be systematically *tested* to be sure it works in all cases. When the program has passed its test, it is ready for use.

The example was so simple that the work could almost have been done faster by hand. But the new program can be embedded in a larger program, for example, in a program that calculates the length of a broken line through a set of several points, or in a program that calculates the perimeter around a cloud of points. The program solves a problem for now and for all future occasions when it may recur.

Into the Writing

The verb write has been reserved to describe the subject of this book because many of the rules of writing good English can be applied to writing good programs. Both an essay and a program have rough drafts and final forms. Both strive for a balance between brevity and clarity. And in both, the rules of style help you polish a rough idea into a smooth result.

The smooth result lives in a social world, but it begins in the creative isolation of the writer. In his isolation all of the rules of good style apply. The rules hold for their practical benefits and for their esthetic pleasure. A well-written program pleases the eye. Writing a program that will meet this standard is a rich problem in its own right and the subject of this book.

To write a program you must comment, code, type, and practice it. The least of these is typing. Yet style begins here because a program reaches the mind's eye through the eye.

TYPING:
ELEMENTARY
KINDNESS
TO
THE
EYE

2

Rule 1

We ought to give the whole of our attention to the most insignificant and most easily mastered facts and remain a long time in contemplation of them until we are accustomed to behold the truth clearly and distinctly.

RENE DESCARTES
Rules for the Direction of the Mind

The first thing you do at the terminal is type in the program. A great deal depends on how you type it in. The speed with which you read a line, the ease with which you understand a block of code, and the amount of time you spend debugging the program are all affected by the clarity of your initial typing. If you pay attention to this dull chore and do it with a little thought you will make your program many times easier to work with.

> **RULE 1**
>
> **Space symbols so that the line may be easily read.**

An unspaced line strains eyes and suffocates meaning. Ventilate a line with space and its symbols can express themselves clearly to the eye.

Weak

```
200 REM ILLEGIBLELINE
201
900 PRINT "PRINTEDRESULTS";R
```

21

Rule 2

Strong

```
200 REM      LEGIBLE LINE
201
900 PRINT "PRINTED RESULTS "; R
```

Even simple lines of familiar words can be improved with good spacing. Both the REM and the PRINT statement benefit from thoughtful typing.

Weak   *Strong*

```
200 LETL=10*(3+4)            200 LET L = 10 * (3+4)
201                          201
400 FOR R=31TOXSTEPS         400 FOR R = 31 TO X STEP S
401                          401
500 IF B>.375 THEN 780       500 IF B > .375 THEN 780
501                          501
600 LET T=3.12456*D          600 LET T = 3.12456 * D
```

The equals sign and other relational operators are easier to read when set off with spaces. A letter used as a variable needs to be separated from the words in a statement. Standard Basic is violated in the bad examples in 200 and 400. All Basic commands must be set off by at least one space. If your version of Basic allows cramped lines, be careful to avoid them.

Weak   *Strong*

```
800 READ A,B,C               800 READ    A,    B,    C
810 DATA 150,175,185         810 DATA 150,  175,  185
```

Sometimes thoughtful spacing can dramatically reveal the meaning of a line. Except where especially noted, even the bad examples in this book are correct Basic statements. Good lines are the result of thinking beyond mere syntax to meaning and form.

RULE 2

End a block of program with a blank line.

Just as sentences are collected around a thought to form a paragraph, lines of code should be collected around an idea to form a block of program. Like a paragraph, a block should be followed by a blank line.

Weak   *Strong*

```
180 REM READ AND TOTAL        100 REM       READ AND TOTAL
200 READ A                    110
210 IF A = -1 THEN 240        120 READ A
220 LET T = T+A               130    IF A = -1 THEN 160
230 GO TO 200                 140       LET T = T + A
240 DATA 4, 3, 5, 7           150 GO TO 120
250 DATA -1                   160
260 PRINT "TOTAL IS "; T      170 DATA 4, 3, 5, 7
                              180 DATA -1
                              190
                              200 PRINT "TOTAL IS "; T
                              210
```

Three ideas yield three blocks of code: a loop that reads and tallies, a set of data, and the printing of results. The three blocks together comprise a program *fragment*, not a whole program.

Standard Basic mistakenly does not require the program to accept a simple blank line. An intelligent version of Basic will permit a blank line. If your version denies you the use of a blank line, use the REM-5 convention described in Rule 3. Most examples in this book will use blank lines, some will use the REM-5 convention.

Weak

```
200 REM STATISTICS
210 FOR I = 1 TO N
220 READ A(I)
230 LET T = T + A(I)
240 NEXT I
250 LET M = T/N
260 LET T = 0
270 FOR I = 1 TO N
280 LET T = T + (A(I)-M)^2
290 NEXT I
300 LET V = T/N
310 LET S = SQR(V)
320 PRINT "MEAN IS "; M
330 PRINT "VARIANCE IS "; V
340 PRINT "STANDARD DEVIATION IS "; S
```

Strong

```
200 REM       STATISTICS
210
220 FOR I = 1 TO N
230    READ A(I)
240      LET T = T + A(I)
250 NEXT I
260
270 LET M = T/N
280
290 LET T = 0
300 FOR I = 1 TO N
310      LET T = T + (A(I)-M)^2
320 NEXT I
330
340 LET V = T/N
350 LET S = SQR(V)
360
370 PRINT "MEAN IS "; M
380 PRINT "VARIANCE IS "; V
390 PRINT "STANDARD DEVIATION IS "; S
400
```

Five ideas, five blocks of code. The line LET M = deserves its own block. Here the arithmetic average (mean) is computed. Lines LET V = and LET S = compute two measures of the spread of the data. A standard statistics text will explain the procedure employed here. These five blocks are not a complete program.

What constitutes a block of code is the writer's decision. What ideas should be set off depends on what the writer seeks to emphasize. No editor who automatically grooms a program according to some of the rules in this book can replace the writer's decisions on block separation or spacing within a line. These considerations are subjective matters of individual judgment.

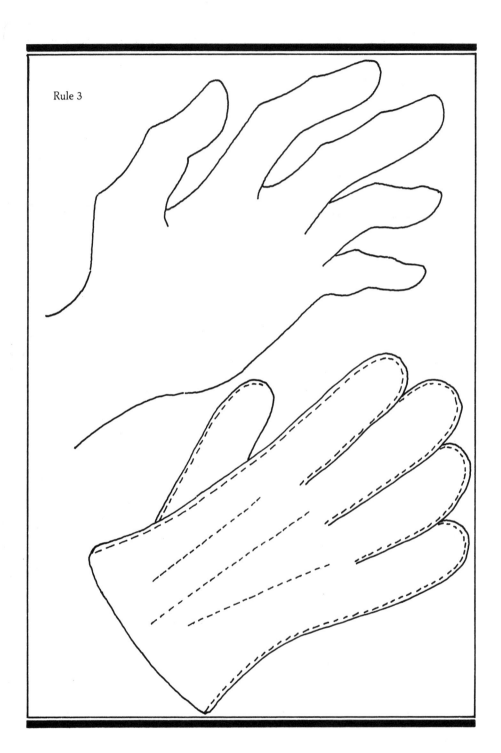

Rule 3

```
                    ┌─────────────────────────────────────┐
                    │              RULE 3                  │
                    │                                      │
                    │    Distinguish comment from code.    │
                    │                                      │
                    └─────────────────────────────────────┘
```

The comment should reveal the code both by what it says and where it says it. The comment should not get in the way. When inserted among lines of code, it should be preceeded and followed with blank lines. Clean code is its own best explanation and good typing should keep the code itself available to the eye.

Weak

```
10 REM CALENDAR LUNATIC
20 REM THIS PART
30 LET M = D/28
40 REM CONVERTS DAYS, D,
50 REM TO MOONS, M, AND
60 REM YEARS, Y.
70 LET Y = M/13
79
```

Strong

```
20 REM      CALENDAR LUNATIC
29
40 REM      THIS PART CONVERTS DAYS, D,
50 REM      TO MOONS, M, AND MOONS TO
60 REM      YEARS, Y.
69
80 LET M = D/28
90 LET Y = M/13
```

Whenever possible, collect dispersed remarks into a paragraph. When this is done in the above example, the eye sees at once that there are only two lines of code, LET M = and LET Y = .

Standard Basic denies the writer an on-line comment. An intelligent version of Basic will overcome this limitation. On-line remarks offer the writer a powerful tool that can be used or misused.

Weak

```
200 REM COMPOUND INTEREST
210
220 LET B = 100 'BEGINNING AMOUNT
230 LET E = 0
235 LET I = 0
240
250 IF E > 170.85 THEN 320
260     LET I = .07 * B 'INTEREST
270     LET E = B + I   'ENDING AMOUNT
280     PRINT B, I, E
290
300     LET B = E 'NEW BEGINNING
310 GO TO 250
320
```

Strong

```
200 REM     COMPOUND INTEREST
210
220 LET B = 100                          'BEGINNING AMOUNT
230 LET E = 0
235 LET I = 0
240
250 IF E > 170.85 THEN 320
260     LET I = .07 * B                  'INTEREST
270     LET E = B + I                    'ENDING AMOUNT
280     PRINT B, I, E
290
300     LET B = E                        'NEW BEGINNING
310 GO TO 250
320
```

When comment is kept well to the right it does not clutter the code. This is as it should be. Comment can sometimes say what the writer thought the code should do, not what the code actually does. The reader has a right to examine the code without being distracted by comment.

On-line remarks can be abused. Use them sparingly. Most remarks are better collected into a paragraph.

Strong

```
200 REM     THIS PART COMPOUNDS INTEREST
210 REM     ON A BEGINNING AMOUNT, B, UNTIL
220 REM     THE ENDING AMOUNT, E, EXCEEDS
230 REM     $ 170.85 .   THE INTEREST RATE
240 REM     IS .07 AND THE RESULTS ARE
250 REM     PRINTED FOR EACH PERIOD.
260'
270 LET B = 100
280 LET E = 0
290 LET I = 0
300
310 IF E > 170.85 THEN 380
320    LET I = .07 * B
330    LET E = B + I
340    PRINT B, I, E
350
360    LET B = E
370 GO TO 310
380
```

The remarks collected into an introductory paragraph explain what the program does and lets the code itself reveal how. Again, the code is kept clean and easy to read.

Weak

```
220 REM THE REM-5 CONVENTION
230 REM
240 REM I1+T1 >= 5,   I2 >= 5.
250 REM
260 REM I1 IS THE REM INDENT
270 REM T1 IS THE TAB FROM REM
280 REM    TO COMMENT.
290 REM I2 IS THE CODE INDENT.
300 REM
310 LET I1 = 1
320 LET T1 = 4
330 LET I2 = 5
340 REM
350 IF I1 <> 1 THEN 410
360 IF T1 < 4 THEN 410
370 IF I2 < 5 THEN 410
380 PRINT "THE REM-5"
390 PRINT "CONVENTION."
400 STOP
410 REM
420 PRINT "CHECK REM FORMAT."
430 REM
```

Rule 4

Strong

```
220 REM      THE REM-5 CONVENTION
230 REM
240 REM      I1+T1 >= 5,   I2 >= 5.
250 REM
260 REM      I1 IS THE REM INDENT
270 REM      T1 IS THE TAB FROM REM
280 REM         TO COMMENT.
290 REM      I2 IS THE CODE INDENT.
300 REM
310      LET I1 = 1
320      LET T1 = 4
330      LET I2 = 5
340 REM
350      IF I1 <> 1 THEN 410
360       IF T1 < 4 THEN 410
370        IF I2 < 5 THEN 410
380         PRINT "THE REM-5"
390         PRINT "CONVENTION."
400          STOP
410 REM
420      PRINT "CHECK REM FORMAT."
430 REM
```

When remarks and blank lines must be REM statements, choose an indent convention that will distinguish comment from code. The REM-5 convention solves the problem. Every example in this book can be written in standard Basic using the REM-5 rule.

```
+-----------------------------------------+
|                 RULE 4                  |
|                                         |
|     Use line numbers of equal length.   |
+-----------------------------------------+
```

Indentation is a potent visual force and poorly chosen line numbers can weaken or destroy indentation's effect.

Weak

```
1 REM      THE SLOPPY CODE
10 REM      WILL SLIP A SPACE
1000 REM      AND OFTEN LOOK A FRIGHT.
```

Strong

```
200 REM       DOGGEREL
210 REM
220 REM       THE SLOPPY CODE
230 REM       WILL SLIP A SPACE
240 REM       AND OFTEN LOOK A FRIGHT.
250 REM
260 REM       THE SLICKER LINES
270 REM       WILL HAVE THE GRACE
280 REM       TO SET THEMSELVES ARIGHT.
290 REM
```

Should your Basic have a resequencer, you will not need to worry about line numbers until you have finished typing. At that time, be sure the line numbers are of equal length.

If you lack a resequencer, number the program between 20 and 90, 200 and 900, or 2000 and 9000 so that later additions can preserve the original numbers' length.

Programs should be written to be as independent of line numbers as possible. Even if you do not resequence your program, someone else may. If the program is styled in a way that does not depend on line numbers it will withstand resequencing. Through careful indentation, Rules 16 and 17 free a Basic program from its dependence on line numbers.

COMMENT:
CLOTHING
THE
NAKED
FORM

3

Rule 5

Clarity is the first aim, economy the second, grace the third.

SHERIDAN BAKER
The Practical Stylist

A computer program is composed of comment and code. Without code the program can not be read by the computer; without comment the program can not be read by a person. A complete program consists of strong code clothed in appropriate comment.

An incomplete program has its occasional uses. A programmer will sometimes dash off a few lines of code, run it once, and throw it away. Such scratch code should not be confused with a complete program. It is a grocery list, not a finished essay.

The complete program will have a head and a body. The head is the introduction and the body is what follows. The body may have several parts, each of which will consist of an introductory remark and blocks of code. Comment's role throughout the program is to introduce the reader to the code. Well tailored remarks will help the reader see whether the code works correctly and whether it suits his or her needs.

The writer of the program is also a reader of the program, so proper comment can help the writer build clean, strong programs. Indeed, when the program's design has been completed, the writer's first step is to put down in plain words what the program will do. Comment follows design and is the first step in writing a computer program.

RULE 5

**Sharpen comment, sharpen code,
sharpen thought.**

Rule 6

Comment precedes, accompanies, and follows code. The comment that precedes the code exemplifies thinking from the general to the particular. When sketching a picture with charcoal, the artist roughs out the general form before delineating the fine detail. Use comment to do the same with a program. Begin with a word sketch of the program's purpose in the introduction. Fill in a few details on the main program with remarks that will explain the blocks of code to follow. Begin to code only after the ideas are roughed out with words.

As the program develops and the code is shaped, comment must be revised to reflect the code. No program ever gets written without a few new twists. These new ideas must be given fit comment. Do not neglect them.

By the time the whole program has been drafted, your understanding of the program has sharpened considerably. Be sure the comment and the code are as sharp as your understanding. Hone the comment as you hone the code.

RULE 6

First draft on paper.

Because the first draft is never perfect, do it on paper. After it has been committed to paper, inadequacies will appear. Comments are rarely as well phrased the first time as they might be. Ways to improve the code appear almost as soon as it is written down. Improvements are easy to make on paper. Not infrequently, the first draft will even suggest a new data structure or a better algorithm.

A final compelling reason for drafting on paper is the almost irresistible urge to jump right into the coding without sketching an outline of comment. If you can not resist the urge to write a few lines of code almost as soon as you hear about an idea for a program, then be sure to do it on paper. You will certainly modify the initial code and it is far easier to play with on paper.

Rule 7

```
┌─────────────────────────────────────┐
│                 RULE 7              │
│                                     │
│             Title to tell.          │
│                                     │
└─────────────────────────────────────┘
```

The first thing the reader encounters is the title of the program. Make it tell. It should be short, apt, and memorable. In conjunction with the first few lines of the introduction, the title should allow the reader to decide whether to quit or to continue. All of the remaining reading will be colored by the title's first impression. Make sure it is the right impression.

Weak		Strong	
REM	FX-3	REM	PLOT
REM	RG14	REM	REGRESS
REM	DICE	REM	CRAPS
REM	CARDS	REM	SHUFFLE

Put the title in the program. Some operating systems do not print it out with each list or run.

Strong

REM	PLOT	1 APRIL 1977	DONALD DUCK
REM	SHUFFLE	1 APRIL 1977	MINNIE MOUSE
REM	CRAPS	1 APRIL 1977	BUGS BUNNY
REM	ID-MB: INDENT MINIMAL BASIC	1 APR 1977	SNOW WHITE
REM	PLOT-FN: PLOT A FUNCTION	1 APR 1977	PORKY PIG

Verbs are stronger titles than nouns. Abbreviations are quite weak. If you must use an abbreviation in the title because of some restriction in the number of permissable characters, be sure to explain the abbreviation on the title line.

Rule 8

```
┌─────────────────────────────────────────────┐
│                                               │
│                    RULE 8                     │
│                                               │
│           Make a formal introduction.         │
│                                               │
└─────────────────────────────────────────────┘
```

A good introduction answers the old newspaper questions: who, what, when, where, and why. Choose a convenient format and use it consistently. Prominently display the title, author's name, and date of origin. In the paragraph that follows, tell what the program does and briefly how. The original introduction is a birth certificate. If the program is altered, the introduction should be amended with the date, author, and details of the alteration. Such a formal pedigree can smooth later maintainance.

Strong

```
100 REM     CRAPS      17 JULY 1977     JOHN M. NEVISON
110
120 REM     PLAY A GAME OF DICE CALLED CRAPS.    ON THE
130 REM     FIRST ROLL WIN WITH A 7 OR 11, LOSE WITH
140 REM     A 2, 3, OR 12, OR GET YOUR "POINT" (4, 5,
150 REM     6, 8, 9, OR 10).   SUBSEQUENT ROLLS,
160 REM     WIN BY MAKING YOUR "POINT" AGAIN,
170 REM     OR LOSE WITH A 7.
180
```

Strong

```
100 REM     EUCLID     17 JULY 1977     JOHN M. NEVISON
110
120 REM     GIVEN TWO POSITIVE WHOLE NUMBERS, D AND N,
130 REM     ARRANGE THEM SO D <= N, AND USING THE
140 REM     EUCLIDEAN ALGORITHM, FIND THEIR GREATEST
150 REM     COMMON DIVISOR, G.
160
```

It is important to give the reader an easy-to-read format that is consistent, so he will know where to look in the next program for the same kind of information.

Rule 9

Strong

```
100 REM     9-SUM      20 JULY 1977     JOHN M. NEVISON
110
115 REM     THIS PROGRAM IS A MODIFICATION OF 7-SUM,
116 REM     (17 JULY 1977 BY JMN).
117
120 REM     IT FINDS THE 9-NUMBER SUMMARY OF A BATCH
130 REM     OF NUMBERS.  BY VARYING THE FUNCTION,
140 REM     FNF(X), ON SUCCESSIVE RUNS,
150 REM     ONE CAN FIND AN EXPRESSION THAT LINES
160 REM     UP THE MID-SPREADS.
170 REM     FUNCTIONS TO TRY INCLUDE:
180 REM     X^2, X^(1/2), LOG(X), -X^(1/2)
190
```

When the program is an adopted child, say so. If its real parentage is known, include it. Even one-page programs benefit by being formally introduced. Six months later anyone can see when the program was written, for what purpose, and by whom. The author's name is critical because when comment fails to explain a mysterious performance, the reader can contact the original programmer. Many a program now waits neglected in the wings because when it misperformed no one knew whom to call to correct it.

RULE 9

Reference critical ideas.

Reference in the strong sense. Provide a full, accurate guide to the journal, book, or professional communication where the idea originated. Santayana cautioned "Those who cannot remember the past are condemned to repeat it." Many ideas in a program are original and some borrowed ideas are too simple to bear mention, but an important idea should reveal its past. If it is correct, the reader has a right to read it in its original form. If it is incorrect, the reader must be given a chance to discover the source of the error. Sometimes an enterprising reader will spot an idea, follow the reference back to the source, and work forward to compose a program tailored to his special needs. Do not deny him his link to the past.

Rule 10

Strong

```
100 REM     REFERENCE:   D.L. SHELL, "A HIGH-SPEED SORTING
115 REM                  PROCEDURE," COMMUNICATIONS OF THE
117 REM                  ACM, VOL. 2, (JULY, 1959) PP.30-32.
120
130 REM     REFERENCE:   J.G. KEMENY, AND T.E. KURTZ, "BASIC
140 REM                  PROGRAMMING," NEW YORK: JOHN WILEY
150 REM                  & SONS,INC., 1971.
160
170 REM     REFERENCE:   JOHN W. TUKEY, "EXPLORATORY DATA
180 REM                  ANALYSIS," READING, MASS: ADDISON-
190 REM                  WESLEY PUBLISHING COMPANY, 1977.
200
```

References may also appear in the body of the program near the algorithm or data structure they explain.

```
┌─────────────────────────────────────┐
│              RULE 10                 │
│                                      │
│      Tag variables and constants     │
│         for quick reference.         │
└─────────────────────────────────────┘
```

Letter abbreviations whose values change are variables; those whose values remain constant are constant labels. Both should be tagged in the introduction. Variables can be listed alphabetically in the introduction while constants should be ordered, labeled and tagged with on-line comments. Both lists should be easy to reference quickly.

Strong

```
100 REM      HISTGRAM         17 JULY 1977      JOHN M. NEVISON
110
120 REM      PRINT A HISTOGRAM OF THE DISTRIBUTION
125 REM      OF N9 RANDOM NUMBERS.
130
140 REM      VARIABLES:
150 REM          H()...THE LENGTH OF EACH HISTOGRAM BAR
160 REM          I.....THE HISTOGRAM INTERVAL
170 REM          J,K...INDEX VARIABLES
180 REM          M.....THE MAXIMUM H()
190 REM          X.....A RANDOM NUMBER
200
210 REM      CONSTANTS:
220      LET H9 = 20         'NUMBER OF HISTOGRAM BARS
230      LET L9 = 35         'LENGTH OF THE LARGEST BAR
240 REM                      '  IN CHARACTERS ACROSS THE PAGE
250      LET N9 = 300        'NUMBER OF RANDOM NUMBERS
260      LET R9 = 3          'NUMBER OF RND'S IN EACH X
270
```

Detailed explanations of variables and constants belong in the body of the program, close to where they appear. Other items that can appear in the introduction include: dimension statements, function definitions, and file declarations. In short, items of program-wide significance are best placed in the introduction.

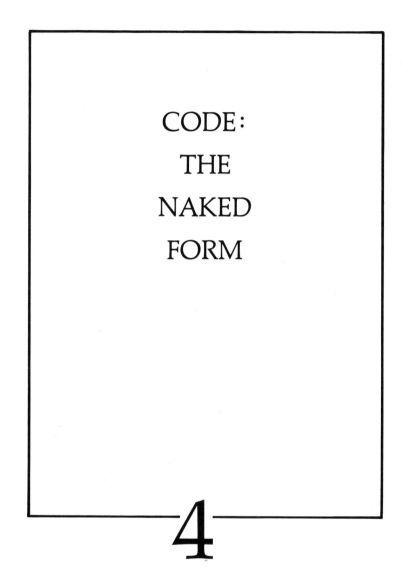

CODE:
THE
NAKED
FORM

4

Recipe language is always a sort of shorthand in which a lot of information is packed, and you will have to read carefully if you are not to miss small but important points.

SIMONE BECK, LOUISETTE BERTHOLLE, JULIA CHILD
Mastering the Art of French Cooking

Imagine for a moment a computer program that contains only comment. A dull, lifeless thing. Add a few lines of code to this comment and the program begins to stir. Continue coding and the program comes to life. Soon a graceful animated form emerges, ready to set about the work of the program. Unfortunately, what sometimes appears is a palsied piece of code, confused by misnamed variables, muddled by poorly expressed lines, itching with unremoved bugs, and puzzled by its own labyrinthine logic. Normal code stands somewhere between these extremes. But the point is clear: the code animates the program.

A healthy program needs healthy code. The program's whole existence is predicated on the assumption that the code works. It must be correct today and robust in the face of tomorrow's changes. Incorrect coding means an incorrect program. An uninitialized variable can begin with a wrong value. A poorly expressed line can conceal a mistake. A badly structured block can misdirect the logical flow of the program. Good coding will make the program easier to read and decrease the initial number of mistakes.

Robust code will withstand rough handling. The code should not be afraid of anything, but it should be cautious in everything. It should check for a wrong number or an error in the logical flow and do something intelligent when such a mistake occurs. To speed the program's repair, lines of code should be carefully pruned so the finished code is easy to inspect. Each part should be exercised as it is completed to make sure that it can withstand abuse.

Sturdy code is usually simple code. Whenever the choice is between a subtle, sophisticated approach and a simple, sure approach, choose the simple.

Rule 11

In simplicity there is strength. Postpone the subtle technique until after the program works and you will probably find it has become unnecessary.

Variables

Code's fundamental element is the variable. Code manipulates variables in expressions and builds these expressions into logical blocks. So a discussion of code must begin with a look at variables.

```
┌─────────────────────────────────────────┐
│                                         │
│               RULE 11                   │
│                                         │
│          Match variables to ideas.      │
│                                         │
└─────────────────────────────────────────┘
```

Select a variable that will be remembered. Associate the variable with the first letter of the object or activity it represents. T is for total, I is for index, D is for data, and X is for xylophones or something special. Spend time to find the right variable and you will be repaid severalfold as you program.

Weak

```
200 REM     THERE ARE A NUMBER, Y9,
210 REM     OF BAGS, X, MIXING
220 REM     APPLES, H, AND ORANGES, S.
230 REM
240         LET H = 0
250         LET S = 0
260         LET X = 0
270
280         FOR V = 1 TO Y9
290             READ H, S
300             LET X = H + S
310             PRINT X
320         NEXT V
330 REM
```

Strong

```
200 REM      THERE ARE A NUMBER, N9,
210 REM      OF BAGS, B, MIXING
220 REM      APPLES,  A, AND ORANGES, O.
230 REM
240      LET A = O
250      LET B = O
260      LET O = O
270
280      FOR I = 1 TO N9
290          READ A, O
300          LET B =  A + O
310          PRINT B
320      NEXT I
330 REM
```

When A is for apple, O is for orange, B is for bag, and N9 is for number, the program's variables are congruent with the program's ideas. (In this discussion, a constant's label can be thought of as a variable.)

Weak

```
200 REM      CIRCLE
209 REM
220      LET R = 3
230      LET Y = R + R
240      PRINT Y,
250      LET Y = 3.14159
260      LET C = 2 * R * Y
270      LET A = Y * R^2
280      PRINT C, A
290 REM
```

Strong

```
100      LET P1 = 3.1415916      'PI
110 REM
120 REM
200 REM      CIRCLE
209 REM
230      LET R = 3
240      LET D = R + R
250      LET C = P1 * D
260      LET A = P1 * R^2
270      PRINT R, D, C, A
280 REM
```

Matching variables to ideas implies that each new idea deserves a distinct variable. In the above example, using Y for both the diameter of the circle and for the constant pi muddles the program. In the stronger version, a reader acquainted with the geometry of a circle might guess that the radius, R, is used to compute the diameter, D, the circumference, C, and the area, A, of a circle. Both examples lack adequate comment.

Certain variables become standardized. Most subscript indices in FOR-NEXT statements are I, J, or K because these letters frequently indicate subscripts in algebra and the convention has carried over to many computer programs. But when the subject of the program turns to insects or jute harvests, other variables will have to serve for subscripts.

Some variables become personal favorites. A mathematician building a sum might use the variable S. An executive accustomed to adding up totals might use the variable T to do the same thing. In either case, a set construction becomes a familiar part of the programming vocabulary.

Strong

```
200        LET T = 0
210        FOR I = 1 TO N
220            LET T = T + D(I)
230        NEXT I
240 REM
250        PRINT "TOTAL IS "; T
260 REM
```

The regular use of I and T matches these variables to certain activities in the program. This association identifies the block at a glance. The reader reads the block as "total the data." A later routine to find another total might safely reuse I and T.

52

D1 ~ Cards in the Deck

3·1415926

π

99

N1 ~ Number of Trials

Rule 12

```
┌─────────────────────────────────────────┐
│              RULE 12                      │
│                                           │
│           Label constants.                │
└─────────────────────────────────────────┘
```

A constant is a number that does not change *during the run of the program*. Its may, however, change between runs. A constant's label is a letter of the alphabet, like a variable, and is sometimes called a parameter. All constants should be labeled in the introduction.

When a constant is labeled at the head of the program the body retains a flexible disposition. When the program needs to do a slightly different task, it can be adapted easily.

Weak

```
200 REM       READ IN
210
220       FOR I = 1 TO 4
230         FOR J = 1 TO 7
240           READ M(I,J)
250         NEXT J
260       NEXT I
270
```

Strong

```
100       LET C9 = 7    'COLUMNS
110       LET R9 = 4    'ROWS
120
130
200 REM       READ IN
210
220       FOR I = 1 TO R9
230         FOR J = 1 TO C9
240           READ M(I,J)
250         NEXT J
260       NEXT I
270
```

An unlabeled constant is no better for a program than candy for a baby. It tastes good going down, but it may lead to a later upset. The example above swallowed a 4 and a 7. With just two sets of FOR-NEXTs the constants cause only a mild stiffness in the two FOR lines. But with several sets in the program, a change in the number of rows would necessitate major surgery. The strong version can expand or contract its rows by simply changing the constant labeled R9. A faster, safer change means a stronger, more versatile piece of code.

Strong

```
210 REM     CONSTANTS:
215     LET L9 = 40      'LENGTH OF THE PLOT IN LINES
220     LET N9 = 50      'NUMBER OF POINTS PLOTTED
225     LET W9 = 72      'WIDTH OF THE PLOT IN CHARS
230     LET X1 = 0       'LEFT BOUNDARY OF PLOT
240     LET X2 = 30      'RIGHT BOUNDARY OF PLOT
250     LET Y1 = 0       'BOTTOM BOUNDARY OF PLOT
260     LET Y2 = 30      'TOP BOUNDARY OF PLOT
290
```

On-line comments are a good way to tag a constant as it is labeled. The value assigned to the constant can also help explain what it is.

Weak

```
200 REM  SPHERES
210
220       LET R = 0
230       LET V = 0
240
250       FOR R = 1 TO 10
260          LET V = 4/3 * 3.14159 * R^3
270             PRINT V
280       NEXT R
290
```

Strong

```
100       LET N9 = 10              'NUMBER
110       LET P1 = 3.1415926       'PI
120
130
200 REM  SPHERES
210
220       LET R = 0
230       LET V = 0
240
250       FOR R = 1 TO N9
260          LET V = 4/3 * P1 * R^3
270             PRINT V
280       NEXT R
290
```

This example swallowed a pi (and a 10). When the constant is labeled once and for all at the head of the program the writer is more likely to type out the full number of digits necessary to span the accuracy of the computer. To do three extra repetitions of the routine, the final number, N9, can be altered in a single LET statement rather than searching through the code looking for every occurrence of a FOR statement.

A small program can be allowed certain constants. For example, a program entitled "Craps" might contain a line that checked to see if the dice roll totaled a losing seven.

Strong

```
100            IF R2 <> 7 THEN 130
110            LET G$ = "LOSE"
120            GO TO 920                    'PRINT OUT
130
```

The constant is as unchanging as the title of the program and the rules of the game. What is lost in versatility is gained in clarity: the reader instantly recognizes the 7.

Several program fragments in this book use unlabeled constants because they are easier to read. If, however, the constant were likely to change, or if the program were larger than one page, or if the constant were to appear several times, it would have to be labeled. In large programs the only unlabeled constants are 0 and 1.

It is good practice to choose a constant's label in a way that distinguishes it from a variable. In this book constant labels will be letter-numeral combinations, for example, N9. Simple letters or subscripted letters, for example, X or A(I,J), will generally be variables.

Rule 13

```
┌─────────────────────────────────────────────┐
│                    RULE 13                    │
│                                               │
│          Initialize a variable near its use.  │
│                                               │
└─────────────────────────────────────────────┘
```

Proximity counts. If a variable is initialized close to its use it is less likely to have a wrong value left over from another part of the program. Placing variables near their use does not require that they be sprinkled one at a time through the code, but that they be grouped in a way convenient to the reader and helpful to the program.

Strong

```
3130 REM     INITIALIZE A CHARACTER POINTER, I, THAT WILL
3135 REM     KEEP TRACK OF HOW FAR THE LINE, L(), HAS BEEN
3140 REM     SEARCHED.
3145
3150 REM     SET POINTERS P1 AND P2 TO THE FIRST AND LAST
3155 REM     DIGITS OF THE LINE NUMBER, N.  STOP WHEN THE
3157 REM     CHARACTER IS NOT A DIGIT BETWEEN 0 (A(48))
3160 REM     AND A 9 (A(57)).
3165
3170     LET I = 1
3175     LET P1 = 1
3180     LET P2 = 0
3185     LET N = 0
3190
3195     IF I >= N9 THEN 3225
3200         IF L(I) < A(48) THEN 3225
3205         IF L(I) > A(57) THEN 3225
3210         LET N = N*10 + FNN(L(I))
3215         LET I = I + 1
3220     GO TO 3195
3225
3230     LET P2 = I-1
3235
```

An index variable may not be initialized if it is always confined to a FOR statement. But when it is used outside a FOR statement, it should be initialized like any other variable.

In small programs, perhaps in most one-page Basic programs, all the variables can be initialized just after the introduction.

Rule 14

Expression

A line of code is more difficult to read than an English sentence. It is terse, abbreviated, and fraught with special symbols. The burden on the reader is heavy in the best of circumstances. Poor expression can crush the reader. The thoughtful programmer can lighten the reader's load by being particularly careful to express each line clearly.

```
RULE 14

Make the line flow left to right.
```

Western language since the time of the Greeks has read left to right, so direction is always lurking behind the order of the line. Take advantage of your reader's predisposition whenever possible.

Weak

```
200 REM       !TFEL OT THGIR
201
300       DATA "LAST", "FIRST", "MIDDLE"
301
400       IF 7 <> R THEN 429
401
500       READ B, A, C
501
600       DEF FNF(X) = 4 + 2*X^2 + 3*X
610
```

Strong

```
200 REM       LEFT TO RIGHT!
201
300       DATA "FIRST", "MIDDLE", "LAST"
301
400       IF R <> 7 THEN 429
401
500       READ A, B, C
501
600       DEF FNF(X) = 2*X^2 + 3*X + 4
610
```

First to last, subject to predicate, A to Z, highest to lowest; whatever the explicit order in a line, it can be strengthened by harmonizing it with the left to right progression of the reader's assimilation.

Rule 15

Almost every IF...THEN can be improved by putting the most varying variable first and comparing it to the least varying variable.

Weak

```
100 REM      MAXIMUM
110
120      FOR I = 1 TO 10
130          IF M > D(I) THEN 150
140            LET M = D(I)
150
160      NEXT I
170
```

Strong

```
100 REM      MAXIMUM
110
120      FOR I = 1 TO 10
130          IF D(I) <  M THEN 150
140            LET M = D(I)
150
160      NEXT I
170
```

RULE 15

Make the line easy to read aloud.

Understanding a line read aloud requires that the line be short or familiar. A complicated expression must be broken into several simple pieces in order to pass the "out loud" test. More than one statement on a line is never allowed.

Weak

```
320 REM      PRESENT VALUE, P, OF A
330 REM      SERIES OF N PAYMENTS OF 1
340 REM      AT AN INTEREST RATE OF
350 REM      I PER PERIOD,
360 REM
370      LET P = (1-(1+I)^(-N))/I
380 REM
```

Strong

```
320 REM       THE PRESENT VALUE, V, OF A
330 REM       SINGLE PAYMENT OF 1 AT
340 REM       PERIOD N WITH AN INTEREST
350 REM       RATE OF I PER PERIOD.
360 REM
370 REM       THE PRESENT VALUE, P, OF
380 REM       A SERIES OF N PAYMENTS OF 1
390 REM       AT AN INTEREST OF I PER PERIOD.
400 REM
410       LET V = 1/(1+I)^N
420       LET P = (1-V)/I
430 REM
```

Weak

```
300 REM       2 THROUGH 9
310 REM
320       IF (X-2) * (9-X) < 0 THEN 350
330        PRINT X ;"WITHIN THE INTERVAL (2,9)."
340         GO TO 370                                'THEN BOTTOM
350 REM
360       PRINT X ;"OUTSIDE THE INTERVAL (2,9)."
370 REM
```

Strong

```
300 REM       2 THROUGH 9
310 REM
320       IF X < 2 THEN 350
325        IF X > 9 THEN 350
330         PRINT X ;"WITHIN THE INTERVAL (2,9)."
340         GO TO 370                                'THEN BOTTOM
350 REM
360       PRINT X ;"OUTSIDE THE INTERVAL (2,9)."
370 REM
```

Weak

```
300 REM       GREAT LEAPS
310 REM
320       IF (X-1968) * (X-1972) * (X-1976) = 0 THEN 340
330        PRINT X; " IS NOT A LEAP YEAR."
340 REM
```

Strong

```
300 REM      GREAT LEAPS
310 REM
320     IF X = 1968 THEN 360
330      IF X = 1972 THEN 360
340       IF X = 1976 THEN 360
350        PRINT X; " IS NOT A LEAP YEAR."
360 REM
```

Complicated expressions in IF...THEN statements frequently obscure their purpose. Re-expressed as several statements, their purpose is clear. The statements below illustrate a good way to handle the logical AND and OR in Minimal Basic.

Strong

```
220 REM      AND
230 REM
240 REM      NEED A AND B AND C TO
250 REM      WIN THE GAME.
260 REM
270     IF A$ <> "YES" THEN 320
280      IF B$ <> "YES" THEN 320
290       IF C$ <> "YES" THEN 320
300        LET G$ = "WIN"
310        PRINT G$
320 REM
```

Strong

```
220 REM      OR
230 REM
240 REM      NEED A OR B OR C TO
250 REM      WIN THE GAME.
260 REM
270     IF A$ = "YES" THEN 310
280      IF B$ = "YES" THEN 310
290       IF C$ = "YES" THEN 310
300        GO TO 340                'THEN BOTTOM
310 REM
320     LET G$ = "WIN"
330     PRINT G$
340 REM
```

Rule 16

Like most of the rules in this book, making the line easy to read aloud is quite subjective. What is easy to read depends on what will be familiar to the reader's ear. As a general rule, assume the reader's background is not above that of an interested novice whose mathematical understanding does not exceed high school algebra. When in doubt, assume less.

Logical Form

Statements must be shaped into sturdy logical structures. As a program grows it can send out tendrils that ensnare its own branches and strangle further growth. A programmer who cautiously prunes the program's logical possibilities at each step can prevent this internal strangulation and encourage further healthy growth.

+---+
| |
| RULE 16 |
| |
| **Code top to bottom.** |
| |
+---+

A convention as old as reading left to right is reading top to bottom. The reader expects to begin the program at the top and end at the bottom. The code should not disappoint him. Each part of the code should have a top and a bottom. Begin the program with a title on the first line and conclude it with an END statement. Begin a subroutine with a title on the first line and end with a RETURN statement. Begin a block of comment or a block of code with the first line and conclude with a blank line.

Weak

```
100 PRINT 2 + 2
110 END
```

Strong

```
120 REM      SUM     23 SEPT  77  JMN
130
140 PRINT 2 + 2
150
160 END
```

Weak

```
340 LET S = A + B
350 RETURN
```

Strong

```
300 REM      SUBROUTINE:  SUM
310 REM        IN:  A, B
320 REM      OUT:  S
330
340      LET S = A + B
350
360 RETURN
```

The program should make sense when read from top to bottom.
Subroutines and blocks of the program should be arranged so the reader going
down the page will encounter them in a convenient order.

Within each block the code itself should also move down the page. To
smooth the logical flow down the page, the IF...THEN and the ON...GO TO
statements should point *down the page*. The IF...THEN should look like this:

Weak   *Strong*

```
10 IF <NOT THE CASE> THEN 40      10 IF <NOT THE CASE> THEN 40
20 CONSEQUENCE                    20    CONSEQUENCE
30 CONSEQUENCE                    30    CONSEQUENCE
40 LINE                           40
50 LINE                           50 LINE
                                  60 LINE
```

The Minimal Basic IF...THEN is always a bit awkward. You may find it
helpful to think of it as saying "If not the case, then skip the consequences." The
consequences may be a short addition to the main flow, a dead end trap for an
error, or a jumping off point to a different part of the program. In every case,
the THEN should point forward down the page to the concluding blank line and
the consequences should reside on indented lines below the IF...THEN.

Weak   *Strong*

```
300 REM      GRADER              300 REM      GRADER
310                              310
320      LET G$ = "F"            320      LET G$ = "F"
330                              330
340      IF S < 70 THEN 420      340      IF S < 70 THEN 400
350       IF S > 79 THEN 380     350      LET G$ = "C"
360        LET G$ = "C"          360      IF S < 80 THEN 400
370        GO TO 420             370      LET G$ = "B"
380       IF S > 89 THEN 410     380      IF S < 90 THEN 400
390        LET G$ = "B"          390      LET G$ = "A"
400        GO TO 420             400
410       LET G$ = "A"           410      PRINT S,G$
420                              420
430      PRINT S,G$
440
```

Weak

```
100 REM     THE ANSWER
110
120     IF A$ = "YES" THEN 150
130     IF A$ = "NO" THEN 170
140     GO TO 190
150     PRINT "THE ANSWER IS YES"
160     GO TO 190
170     PRINT "THE ANSWER IS NO"
180     GO TO 190
190     PRINT A$
```

Strong

```
100 REM     THE ANSWER
110
120     IF A$ <> "YES" THEN 150
130      PRINT "THE ANSWER IS YES"
140      GO TO 200
150
160     IF A$ <> "NO" THEN 190
170      PRINT "THE ANSWER IS NO"
180      GO TO 200
190
200     PRINT A$
210
```

All IF...THENs should form structures as self-contained as sleeping cats. Their logical tails should be tucked in under them. The advantages of this form are many. One can quickly see where the unskipped condition ends and the main program continues. Because the THEN statement is tucked into the blank line at the bottom of the construction, the IF...THEN forms become self-contained blocks and can be stacked with assurance. Daisy chains of IF...THENs do not exist.

Each of an ON...GO TO's line numbers should point down the page to a REM title for each block of code. Each block should finish by going to the ON...GO TO's bottom blank line.

Strong

```
100 REM      SEVEN DWARVES
110
120          ON D THEN 140, 190, 240, 290, 340, 390, 440,
130
140 REM      CASE 1
150
160          PRINT "GRUMPY"
170          GO TO 480                              'ON BOTTOM
180
190 REM      CASE 2
200
210          PRINT "DOC"
220          GO TO 480                              'ON BOTTOM
230
240 REM      CASE 3
250
260          PRINT "SNEEZY"
270          GO TO 480                              'ON BOTTOM
280
290 REM      CASE 4
300
310          PRINT "BASHFUL"
320          GO TO 480                              'ON BOTTOM
330
340 REM      CASE 5
350
360          PRINT "SLEEPY"
370          GO TO 480                              'ON BOTTOM
380
390 REM      CASE 6
400
410          PRINT "HAPPY"
420          GO TO 480                              'ON BOTTOM
430
440 REM      CASE 7
450
460          PRINT "DOPEY"
470          GO TO 480                              'ON BOTTOM
480
```

The loop, a set of repeated instructions, interrupts the reader's movement down the page. So a loop is inherently difficult to read. Because many of a program's logical difficulties are associated with loops, this meeting ground of logical complexity and reading difficulty is of critical importance to the health of a program. Even Minimal Basic provides enough statements to ensnare the unwary programmer in a confusion of loops.

The model for a good loop is the FOR-NEXT pair.

Weak	*Strong*

```
10 FOR I = 1 TO 10          10 FOR I = 1 TO 10
20 LINE                     20    LINE
30 LINE                     30    LINE
40 LINE                     40    LINE
50 NEXT I                   50 NEXT I
```

When the loop is properly indented, the structure leaps to the eye: a top, an indented middle, and a bottom. A loop may also be constructed with a GO TO.

Weak	*Strong*

```
10 LINE                     10 LINE
20 LINE                     20    LINE
30 LINE                     30    LINE
40 LINE                     40    LINE
50 GO TO 10                 50 GO TO 10
```

The GO TO loop is not as well defined as a FOR-NEXT and is not at all visible without its indented middle. The loop indentation is the most important indentation in the code. It should be at least *three spaces deep.*

Weak	*Strong*

```
200 REM      TALLY DATA     200 REM      TALLY DATA
210                         210
220       LET T = 0         220       LET T = 0
230       FOR I = 1 TO N    230       FOR I = 1 TO N
240       READ D(I)         240          READ D(I)
250       LET T = T + D(I)  250          LET T = T + D(I)
260       PRINT D(I),T      260          PRINT D(I),  T
270       NEXT I            270       NEXT I
279                         279
```

You should be able to tell at a glance whether a piece of code is a section that might be skipped (IF...THEN) or a section that might be repeated (loop). So if the IF...THEN indent is three, then the loop should should be five.

Rule 17

Weak   *Strong*

```
100 REM     FACTORIAL          100 REM       FACTORIAL
110                            110
120 LET F = 1                  120      LET F = 1
130 IF N <> 0 THEN 160         130      IF N <> 0 THEN 160
140 PRINT F                    140       PRINT F
150 STOP                       150        STOP
160 FOR I = 1 TO N             160
170 LET F = F * I              170      FOR I = 1 TO N
180 NEXT I                     180        LET F = F * I
190 PRINT F                    190      NEXT I
200 STOP                       200      PRINT F
                               210      STOP
```

```
┌─────────────────────────────────────────┐
│                                         │
│              RULE 17                     │
│                                         │
│     Nest structures that work together.  │
│                        .                │
└─────────────────────────────────────────┘
```

If two structures work together at the same time on the same task, they should be nested. The first structure should start first and finish last. The best example of this rule is the program itself. The program works together with every structure within it and its title line starts first and its END statement finishes last.

The common example of cooperating structures in a program is a pair of loops. If each loop is given its normal indentation, the pair's logical nesting is clear to the reader.

Weak   *Strong*

```
10 REM     MATRIX READ         10 REM       MATRIX READ
20                             20
30 FOR I = 1 TO 4              30      FOR I = 1 TO 4
40 FOR J = 1 TO 7              40        FOR J = 1 TO 7
50 READ M(I,J)                 50          READ M(I,J)
60 NEXT J                      60        NEXT J
70 NEXT I                      70      NEXT I
80                             80
```

IF...THENs also work together often.

Weak

```
100 REM       MORAL QUESTION
110
120 IF M$ <> "AVOID EVIL" THEN 180
130 IF V$ <> "TRY TO DO GOOD" THEN 160
140 PRINT "MORAL AND VIRTUOUS"
150 GO TO 190
160 PRINT "MORAL"
170 GO TO 190
180 PRINT "IMMORAL"
190
```

Strong

```
100 REM       MORAL QUESTION
110
120       IF M$ <> "AVOID EVIL" THEN 190
130        IF V$ <> "TRY TO DO GOOD" THEN 160
140         PRINT "MORAL AND VIRTUOUS"
150         GO TO 210                        'QUESTION BOTTOM
160
170         PRINT "MORAL"
180         GO TO 210                        'QUESTION BOTTOM
190
200       PRINT "IMMORAL"
210
```

Loops and IF...THENs can also work with each other. When each is given its own proper indentation, the logic of their nesting structures is quickly revealed.

Weak

```
200 REM LARGEST LAST
210
220       FOR I = 1 TO N9-1
230       IF D(I) <= D(I+1) THEN 280
250        LET X = D(I)
260        LET D(I) = D(I+1)
270        LET D(I+1) = X
280
290       NEXT I
300
```

Strong

```
200 REM      LARGEST LAST
210
220      FOR I = 1 TO N9-1
230          IF D(I) <= D(I+1) THEN 280
240            LET X = D(I)
260            LET D(I) = D(I+1)
270            LET D(I+1) = X
280
290      NEXT I
300
```

Weak

```
200 REM      BUBBLE SORT
210
220      FOR L = N TO 2 STEP -1
230      FOR I = 1 TO L-1
240      IF D(I) <= D(I+1) THEN 290
250      LET X = D(I)
270      LET D(I) = D(I+1)
280      LET D(I+1) = X
290
300      NEXT I
310      NEXT L
320
```

Strong

```
200 REM      BUBBLE SORT
210
220      FOR L = N TO 2 STEP -1
230          FOR I = 1 TO L-1
240              IF D(I) <= D(I+1) THEN 290
250                LET X = D(I)
270                LET D(I) = D(I+1)
280                LET D(I+1) = X
290
300          NEXT I
310      NEXT L
320
```

Rule 18

Weak

```
100 REM      NUMBER OF ASTERISKS
110
120 IF N <= 0 THEN 170
130 FOR I = 1 TO N
140 PRINT "*";
150 NEXT I
160 PRINT
170 PRINT "DONE"
180
```

Strong

```
100 REM      NUMBER OF ASTERISKS
110
120     IF N <= 0 THEN 170
130       FOR I = 1 TO N
140           PRINT "*";
150       NEXT I
160       PRINT
170
180     PRINT "DONE"
190
```

The indentation reveals the nesting clearly in all three examples.

```
┌─────────────────────────────────────────┐
│                 RULE 18                   │
│                                           │
│              Exit carefully.              │
│                                           │
└─────────────────────────────────────────┘
```

Even when every structure is entered correctly at the top, the reader can be completely confounded by careless exits. The code should exit carefully so the reader can quickly grasp the structure of the code. Each exit should be clearly marked and point down the page.

In Minimal Basic most exits are made with a GO TO. When a GO TO statement exits, it should say precisely where it is going with an on-line comment. If you are denied on-line comments, mark your GO TO's with pseudo on-line REM lines immediately after the GO TO. In most cases one REM line can serve both as a pseudo blank line and as a pseudo on-line comment.

Weak   *Strong*

```
310 GO TO 800                    310 GO TO 800      'LAST PART
```

Weak   *Strong*

```
310 GO TO 800                    310        GO TO 800
320 REM                          320 REM                    'LAST PART
```

Strong

```
250 REM      EXIT TO NEW PART 800
260
270      IF A$ <> "YES" THEN 320
280       IF B$ <> "YES" THEN 320
290        IF C$ <> "YES" THEN 320
300         LET G$ = "WIN"
310         GO TO 800                         'PRINT OUT
320
330      LET G$ = "CONTINUE"
340
```

Strong

```
200 REM      EXIT TO BOTTOM OF STRUCTURE
210
220      IF INT(N/2) <> N/2 THEN 250
230       PRINT "EVEN NUMBER IS "; N
240       GO TO 270                          'THEN BOTTOM
250
260      PRINT "ODD NUMBER IS "; N
270
```

A clearly marked exit helps the reader see where the GO TO is going, but it is
also extremely important that the GO TO point down the page.

Weak

```
200 REM      INPUT CHECK
210
220      PRINT "PLEASE ENTER A NUMBER FROM 4 TO 16 ";
230      INPUT N
239
240      IF N = INT(N) THEN 270
250       PRINT "PLEASE TYPE IN AN INTEGER."
260       GO TO 220                          'INPUT CHECK
270      IF N >= 4 THEN 300
280      PRINT "NUMBER MUST BE 4 OR MORE."
290      GO TO 220                           'INPUT CHECK
300      IF N <= 16 THEN 330
310       PRINT "NUMBER MUST BE 16 OR LESS."
320       GO TO 220                          'INPUT CHECK
330      PRINT TAB ((N-4)/12 * 72); "*"
```

Strong

```
100 REM      INPUT CHECK
110
120      PRINT "PLEASE ENTER A NUMBER FROM 4 TO 16 ";
130        INPUT N
140
150        IF N = INT(N) THEN 180
160          PRINT "PLEASE TYPE IN AN INTEGER."
170          GO TO 280                               'LOOP BOTTOM
180
190        IF N >= 4 THEN 220
200          PRINT "NUMBER MUST BE 4 OR MORE."
210          GO TO 280                               'LOOP BOTTOM
220
230        IF N <= 16 THEN 260
240          PRINT "NUMBER MUST BE 16 OR LESS."
250          GO TO 280                               'LOOP BOTTOM
260
270          GO TO 290                               'LOOP EXIT
280      GO TO 120
290
300      PRINT TAB ((N-4)/12 * 72); "*"
```

By making the exits all point down the page, a hidden loop was forced out in the open. By exiting carefully down the page, the GO TO smooths the program's flow from top to bottom.

By making a three-line conditional exit with an IF...THEN, a GO TO, and a blank line, a programmer can always exit with a GO TO.

Strong

```
370 IF <NOT THE EXIT CASE> THEN 390
380   GO TO 560      'NEXT PART
390
```

Using this three line exit is a good practice in general, but it can obscure the program's logic in certain cases.

Weak

```
200 REM      TOTAL
210
240      IF  A <> -1  THEN  248
242          GO  TO  280
248
249          LET  T = T + A
250          READ  A
270      GO  TO  240
280
```

Strong

```
200 REM      TOTAL
210
240      IF  A = -1  THEN  280
249          LET  T = T + A
250          READ  A
270      GO  TO  240
280
```

Weak

```
100 REM      FIND  NEXT  SPACE  (ASCII  32)
110
120      IF  I < N  THEN  140
130          GO  TO  200
140
150          IF  L(I) <> 32  THEN  170
160            GO  TO  200
170
180          LET  I = I + 1
190      GO  TO  120
200
```

Strong

```
100 REM      FIND  NEXT  SPACE  (ASCII  32)
110
120      IF  I >= N  THEN  200
150          IF  L(I) = 32  THEN   200
180            LET  I = I + 1
190      GO  TO  120
200
```

In all the examples, weak and strong, loop indentation takes precedence over IF...THEN indentation, so the loop's structure will remain clear. Exiting from the loop, however, is less clear in the weak examples. In the strong examples, the reader senses that the IF...THEN exits the loop because the loop does not contain the blank line that forms the bottom of an IF...THEN.

Because an exiting IF...THEN violates Rule 17 as it crosses the bottom of a loop, it should only be used in very restricted circumstances. An IF...THEN may exit a loop only when it occurs at the very top or very bottom of a loop, never in the middle, and only when it remains nested within the other IF...THENs. An IF...THEN should never violate its nesting with another IF...THEN.

The GO SUB does not exit, it takes a leave, an officially approved absence. When it returns from leave the program continues with the next line.

The GO SUB, however, like the GO TO, should say where it is going in an on-line comment.

Weak

```
375 GO SUB 800
```

Strong

```
375 GO SUB 800          'PRINT OUT
```

If the subroutine has been titled to tell, the reader will understand roughly what the subroutine is supposed to do, defer the details until a later reading of the subroutine, and continue the primary journey down the page.

Rule 19

RULE 19

Practice the program, exercise and proofread.

A program should be given practice runs and practice reads. Whenever convenient, exercise a completed block of code to be sure it works. If exercise becomes a habit, errors become isolated in time as well as in position on the page. When the program does not work, the error is likely to be in the most recently written code. By writing the code a piece at a time and exercising each piece, you can quickly diagnose and correct errors. Exercise builds strong code.

A writer always asks someone else to proofread his work to be sure it reads clearly and is free of errors. A program's writer should do the same. Code can be checked by exercising it on the computer. Comment must be checked by allowing a new reader to make his way through it. A fresh point of view can detect comment's most frequent sin: omission. Proofreading ensures that the code is well dressed in comment.

Both forms of practice, proofreading and exercise, are necessary for a healthy program. Omit either and the program will suffer.

EXAMPLES:
THE
PROGRAM
AT
WORK
AND
PLAY

5

A foolish consistency is the hobgoblin of little minds.

RALPH WALDO EMERSON
Self Reliance

All of the foregoing rules of style are bracketed by two important unwritten rules. The rule that precedes all others is *follow the rule before breaking it*. If the writer observes a rule long enough to grow accustomed to it, he may find that it actually speeds the writing of the program. Try the tool before discarding it.

The unwritten rule that succeeds all others is *when there is good reason, break the rule*. Good reason must be an argument for clarity, ease of reading, or, weakest of all, brevity. Bad reason includes every argument about machine storage and processor efficiency. Machine storage is cheap. Arguments about efficiency, until they are supported with instrumented runs that show where a program is truly inefficient, remain mere excuses.

A program's comment clothes a program's code. As with clothing, what comment a program should wear depends on where it is. At home, if the program finds itself cramped for space by a long introduction, it might well lay the introduction neatly aside before it begins to work. It should not lose its introduction, however, because later when it wants to go visiting it will want to don proper attire before stepping out.

On a long trip a program might well take along a suitcase of extra comment. This second file might contain a sample of the program as it is run, both its input and output. It might contain detailed instruction on its use in strange enviornments, notes on code that was not standard, and warnings about its intended use and limitations. It might have extra directions on where to write and whom to call if the program gets in trouble. This telephone number is very important. The fastest way to get a traveling program straightened out is to call the program's original author.

The following programs are fully dressed, but without suitcases. Most are one page long. All have been carefully styled according to the rules in this book. They aim to illustrate the rules of style in a variety of ways. Runs of each program are included to show what it does. The run is intended to *supplement* the program's own comment and code, not to *substitute* for them.

MIX illustrates itself with a simple batch of numbers. The strength of the three central lines of the program where I1 appears is that each line can be read as a physical move: first pick a card, then move it to the shuffled (mixed) deck, then move the end card into the hole in the unshuffled deck.

The body for the program contains three clearly defined loops that correspond to: read in, process, and write out.

The subroutine , SHUFFLE, in the program, CARDDEAL, shows how to write MIX using only one subscripted variable for the batch of numbers.

```
MIX        16 SEP 77    14:06

10   20   30   40   50   60   70   80   90   100
110  120  130  140  150  160  170  180  190  200
210  220  230  240  250  260  270  280  290  300
310  320  330  340  350  360  370  380  390  400
410  420  430  440  450  460  470  480  490  500
510  520


380  450  370  80   60   310  150  480  70   440
360  410  500  280  250  190  420  160  270  260
390  340  520  20   510  30   230  470  180  50
290  460  400  10   130  200  90   240  110  100
40   320  490  350  170  120  330  210  300  430
140  220
```

```
100 REM     MIX                        17 JULY 1977          JOHN M. NEVISON
110
120 REM     MIXES UP A BATCH OF NUMBERS B(), TO PRODUCE A MIXED
130 REM     BATCH, M().  THIS PROGRAM COULD ALSO HAVE BEEN TITLED
140 REM     SCRAMBLE OR SHUFFLE.
150
160 REM     VARIABLES:
170 REM         B()...THE BATCH OF NUMBERS
180 REM         I.....INDEX VARIABLE
190 REM         I1....MIXED INDEX VARIABLE
200 REM         M()...THE MIXED BATCH OF NUMBERS
210
220 REM     CONSTANTS:
230     LET N9 = 52                          'NUMBER IN BATCH
240
250 REM     DIMENSIONS:
260     DIM B(52), M(52)
270
280 REM     MAIN PROGRAM
290
300 REM     READ IN THE BATCH AND INITIALIZE M() AND I1.
310 REM     SHUFFLE THE BATCH BY PICKING ONE AT A TIME AND
320 REM     MOVING IT TO THE MIXED BATCH, AND PRINT OUT THE
330 REM     MIXED BATCH
340
350     LET I1 = 0
360     FOR I = 1 TO N9
370        LET M(I) = 0
380     NEXT I
390
400     FOR I = 1 TO N9
410        LET B(I) = I * 10
420        PRINT B(I);
430     NEXT I
440     PRINT
450     PRINT
460
470     FOR I = N9 TO 1 STEP -1
480        LET I1 = INT(RND*I + 1)
490        LET M(I) = B(I1)
500        LET B(I1) = B(I)
510     NEXT I
520
530     FOR I = 1 TO N9
540        PRINT M(I);
550     NEXT I
560     PRINT
570
580     END
```

SORT undoes MIX. Using a selection sort, it arranges a small batch of numbers in ascending order by putting the largest last on each successive pass through the unsorted batch.

```
100 REM     SORT              16 SEPTEMBER 1977   JOHN M. NEVISON
110
120 REM     SORTS A MIXED BATCH OF NUMBERS, B(), INTO ASCENDING
130 REM     ORDER.  ESPECIALLY GOOD FOR BATCHES OF LESS THAN 50.
140
150 REM     VARIABLES:
160 REM         B()...THE BATCH OF NUMBERS
170 REM         I.....THE INDEX VARIABLE
180 REM         L.....THE LENGTH OF THE CURRENT LIST
190 REM         X.....THE EXCHANGE VARIABLE
200
210 REM     CONSTANT:
220     LET N9 = 38                          'NUMBER OF DATA
230
240 REM     DIMENSIONS:
250     DIM B(38)
260
270 REM     MAIN PROGRAM
280
290 REM     READ IN N9 RANDOM NUMBERS, SORT THEM,
300 REM     AND PRINT THEM OUT.
310
315     LET X = 0
320     FOR I = 1 TO N9
330         LET B(I) = INT(RND*25 +1)
340         PRINT B(I);
350     NEXT I
360     PRINT
366     PRINT
370
380     FOR L = N9 TO 2 STEP -1
390         FOR I = 1 TO L-1
400             IF B(I) <= B(L) THEN 440
410             LET X = B(I)
420             LET B(I) = B(L)
430             LET B(L) = X
440
450         NEXT I
460     NEXT L
470
480     FOR I = 1 TO N9
490         PRINT B(I);
500     NEXT I
510     PRINT
520
530     END
```

```
SORT      16 SEP 77  14:50

 11   7   22   15   11   18   7   10   20   18
 19   3    7    7   16    7  14   10    1    7
  9  24    4   15    9   22   3   14    2   24
  1  13    3    1   22   18   1   23

  1   1    1    1    2    3   3    3    4    7
  7   7    7    7    7    9   9   10   10   11
 11  13   14   14   15   15  16   18   18   18
 19  20   22   22   22   23  24   24
```

Programs do not need to be long or complicated to be useful. PRESENT does a calculation frequently encountered in financial work. Because the program is so short, it can be read quickly and used repeatedly.

```
100 REM      PRESENT              17JULY 1977        JOHN M. NEVISON
110
120 REM      COMPUTE THE PRESENT VALUE, V, OF A FUTURE SERIES OF
130 REM      PAYMENTS, P(), AT A RATE OF RETURN, R9.
140
150 REM      BY VARYING THE RATE OF RETURN, R9, THE USER MAY DETERMINE
160 REM      WHAT VALUE YIELDS THE PRESENT COST.  THIS RATE IS SOMETIMES
170 REM      CALLED THE INTERNAL RATE OF RETURN.
180
190 REM      VARIABLES:
200 REM          F...THE DISCOUNT FACTOR
210 REM          I...INDEX VARIABLE
220 REM          P().THE PAYMENTS
230 REM          V...THE PRESENT VALUE OF THE STRING OF PAYMENTS.
240
250 REM      CONSTANTS:
260      LET R9 = 20               'RATE OF RETURN (%)
270      LET N9 = 5                'NUMBER OF PAYMENTS
280
290 REM      MAIN PROGRAM
300
310      LET F = 1/(1 + R9/100)
315      LET V = 0
320
330      FOR I = 1 TO N9
340         READ P(I)
350      NEXT I
360      DATA 5,10,10,15,200000
370
380      FOR I = 1 TO N9
390         LET V = V + F^I * P(I)
400      NEXT I
410
411      PRINT "FOR THE SERIES OF FUTURE PAYMENTS "
412      FOR I = 1 TO N9
413         PRINT I;P(I)
414      NEXT I
415      PRINT
417
420      PRINT "PRESENT VALUE AT "; R9;"% RETURN IS "; V ;" ."
430
440      END
```

```
   PRESENT   16 SEP 77  15:23

FOR THE SERIES OF FUTURE PAYMENTS
  1   5
  2   10
  3   10
  4   15
  5   200000

PRESENT VALUE AT  20 % RETURN IS  80399.6  .
```

BIG-SORT illustrates an algorithm that sorts more that fifty items faster than the simple selection sort. For illustration, it generates fifty-five numbers, sorts them, and prints out the results. Explaining how the program works is left to the code itself. The reader may work through the code and may refer to the original source. Either is preferable to a verbose explanation of a complicated idea.

The code itself is clear. Variables are initialized, loops are clearly indented, IF...THENs are indented and concluded with blank lines. Note how loop indentation takes precedence over IF...THEN indentation.

```
BIG-SORT   16 SEP 77   15:02

11   7   22   15   11   18   7   10   20   18
19   3   7    7    16   7    14  10   1    7
9    24  4    15   9    22   3   14   2    24
1    13  3    1    22   18   1   23   18   10
7    6   12   20   8    18   3   1    13   1
12   7   7    19   11

1    1   1    1    1    1    2   3    3    3
3    4   6    7    7    7    7   7    7    7
7    7   8    9    9    10   10  10   11   11
11   12  12   13   13   14   14  15   15   16
18   18  18   18   18   19   19  20   20   22
22   22  23   24   24
```

```
100 REM     BIG-SORT         17 JULY 1977       JOHN M. NEVISON
110
120 REM     SORTS A MIXED BATCH OF NUMBERS, B(), INTO ASCENDING
130 REM     ORDER.  ESPECIALLY GOOD FOR BATCHES OF MORE THAN 50.
140
150 REM     REFERENCE:  D.L. SHELL, COMMUNICATIONS OF THE ACM,
160 REM                 VOL 2, (JULY, 1959), PP. 30-32.
170
180 REM     VARIABLES:
190 REM         B()...THE BATCH OF NUMBERS
200 REM         E$....EXCHANGE MARKER
210 REM         G.....THE GAP
220 REM         I.....INDEX VARIABLE
230 REM         S.....THE STEP ACROSS THE GAP
240 REM         T.....THE TOP OF THE PASS THROUGH THE NUMBERS
250 REM         X.....EXCHANGE VARIABLE
260
270 REM     CONSTANT:
280         LET N9 = 55                        'NUMBER OF DATA
290
300 REM     DIMENSIONS:
310         DIM B(55)
320
330 REM     MAIN PROGRAM
340
350 REM     COMPARES ITEMS ACROSS A GAP N9/2 WIDE UNTIL THERE ARE NO
360 REM     MORE EXCHANGES, THEN CUTS THE GAP IN HALF AND REPEATS.
370
380         FOR I = 1 TO N9
390            LET B(I) = INT(RND*25 + 1)
400            PRINT B(I);
410         NEXT I
420         PRINT
430         PRINT
440
450         LET E$ = " "
460         LET S = 0
470         LET T = 0
480         LET X = 0
490         LET G = N9
500
510         IF G <= 1 THEN 680
520            LET G = INT(G/2)
530            LET T = N9 - G
540            LET E$ = "NO EXCHANGE"
550               FOR I = 1 TO T
560                  LET S = I + G
570                  IF B(I) <= B(S) THEN 620
580                  LET X = B(I)
590                  LET B(I) = B(S)
600                  LET B(S) = X
610                  LET E$ = "EXCHANGE"
620
630               NEXT I
640               IF E$ = "NO EXCHANGE" THEN 660
650            GO TO 540
660
670         GO TO 510
680
690         FOR I = 1 TO N9
700            PRINT B(I);
710         NEXT I
720         PRINT
730
740         END
```

EUCLID illustrates a famous algorithm for finding the greatest common factor of two numbers. Details can be found in any high school algebra text.

The program checks the input very carefully before it goes on to work with it. Both checks use IF...THENs together in their logical OR form. The checks are embedded in a GO TO loop that returns to the question until it is answered correctly.

The main program itself solves another interesting problem for the writer of a well styled program. The variables Q and R are figured before one can check R to see if things are finished. If more work remains, two lines of code are necessary to reinitialize N and D for another try. The IF...THEN is in the middle of what might be a loop. Because IF...THENs should only exit loops from the top or the bottom, two extra lines are added to make a loop out of all subsequent calculations.

```
EUCLID     16 SEP 77   15:41

PLEASE TYPE IN TWO POSITIVE, WHOLE NUMBERS? 12,-1
PLEASE MAKE SURE BOTH NUMBERS ARE POSITIVE.
PLEASE TYPE IN TWO POSITIVE, WHOLE NUMBERS? 5,9.2
PLEASE MAKE SURE BOTH NUMBERS ARE WHOLE NUMBERS.
PLEASE TYPE IN TWO POSITIVE, WHOLE NUMBERS? 9,12
GREATEST COMMON FACTOR IS   3
```

```
100 REM     EUCLID              17 JULY 1977         JOHN M. NEVISON
110
120 REM     GIVEN TWO POSITIVE WHOLE NUMBERS, D AND N, ARRANGE
130 REM     THEM SO D <= N, AND USING THE EUCLIDEAN ALGORITHM,
140 REM     FIND THEIR GREATEST COMMON DIVISOR, G.
150
160 REM     VARIABLES:
170 REM         D,N..DENOMINATOR AND NUMERATOR, THE TWO NUMBERS
180 REM         Q....QUOTIENT OF THE TWO NUMBERS
190 REM         R....THE REMAINDER AFTER THE DIVISION
200 REM         X..:.EXCHANGE VARIABLE
210
220 REM     INPUT AND CHECK
230
240     PRINT "PLEASE TYPE IN TWO POSITIVE, WHOLE NUMBERS";
250         INPUT D,N
260
270         IF D <= 0 THEN 300
280         IF N <= 0 THEN 300
290           GO TO 330                   'THEN BOTTOM
300
310         PRINT "PLEASE MAKE SURE BOTH NUMBERS ARE POSITIVE."
320         GO TO 394                     'LOOP BOTTOM
330
340         IF D <> INT(D) THEN 370
350         IF N <> INT(N) THEN 370
360           GO TO 400                   'THEN BOTTOM
370
380         PRINT "PLEASE MAKE SURE BOTH NUMBERS ARE WHOLE NUMBERS."
390         GO TO 394                     'LOOP BOTTOM
391
392         GO TO 400                     'LOOP EXIT
394     GO TO 240
400
410     LET X = 0
420     IF D <= N THEN 460
430         LET X = D
440         LET D = N
450         LET N = X
460
470 REM     MAIN PROGRAM
480
490     LET Q = INT( N/D )
500     LET R = N - Q*D
510     IF R = 0 THEN 570
520         LET N = D
530         LET D = R
540         LET Q = INT( N/D )
550         LET R = N - Q*D
560     GO TO 510
570
580     PRINT "GREATEST COMMON FACTOR IS "; D
590     END
```

CRAPS is a program at play. One of the very appealing features of Basic is how it can be used to explain an idea. Here the program itself is the explanation of the rules of the game.

Two variables are initialized before the first roll and the remaining three variables are initialized immediately after.

The IF...THEN leading the two ON statements is really a part of a three-line construction so the THEN does not point to a blank line. The ON itself points to one of three blocks, each of which begins with a REM title.

```
CRAPS      16 SEP 77   15:51

WIN
```

```
100 REM     CRAPS            17 JULY 1977        JOHN M. NEVISON
110
120 REM     PLAY A GAME OF DICE CALLED CRAPS.  ON THE FIRST ROLL
130 REM     WIN WITH 7 OR 11, LOSE WITH 2, 3, OR 12, OR GET YOUR
140 REM     "POINT" (4, 5, 6, 8, 9, OR 10).  SUBSEQUENT ROLL,
150 REM     WIN BY MAKING YOUR "POINT" AGAIN, LOSE WITH A 7.
160
170 REM     VARIABLES:
180 REM         D(1),D(2)...THE OUTCOME OF THE TWO DICE
190 REM         G$............THE GAME STATE
200 REM         R(1),R(2).....THE ROLL OF THE DICE
210
220 REM     MAIN PROGRAM
230
240     LET G$ = "BEGIN"
250     LET R(2) = 0
260
270 REM     FIRST ROLL
280
290     LET D(1) = INT(RND*6 + 1)
300     LET D(2) = INT(RND*6 + 1)
310     LET R(1) = D(1) + D(2)
320
330     IF R(1) > 6 THEN 350
340     ON R(1) GO TO 630, 420, 420, 470, 470, 470
350     ON R(1) -6 GO TO 340, 370, 470, 470, 470, 370, 420
360
370 REM     WIN ON 7, 11.
380
390     LET G$ = "WIN"
400     GO TO 630                        'RESULTS
410
420 REM     LOSE ON 2, 3, 12.
430
440     LET G$ = "LOSE"
450     GO TO 630                        'RESULTS
460
470 REM     SUBSEQUENT ROLL(S)
480
490     LET D(1) = INT(RND*6 + 1)
500       LET D(2) = INT(RND*6 + 1)
510       LET R(2) = D(1) + D(2)
520
530       IF R(2) <> 7 THEN 560
540       LET G$ = "LOSE"
550       GO TO 630                      'RESULTS
560
570       IF R(2) <> R(1) THEN 600
580       LET G$ = "WIN"
590       GO TO 630                      'RESULTS
600
610     GO TO 490
620
630 REM     RESULTS
640     PRINT G$
650     END
```

PLOT is a utility program that can be used in a variety of ways. As it exists, it generates random points and then plots them, but it could be modified to handle points from another part of a larger program. When a small program is carefully written, it can frequently be used in more than one context.

The program labels seven constants. If a stranger wanted to use this program, but wanted to spread the graph over the full width of a 72 character page, he could do it quickly and with confidence by altering W9 and its accompanying DIM. Because all the constants are labeled, the program is easy to modify for these new uses.

The program transforms X and Y to indicies of the G matrix in two steps so that both lines will be easy to read aloud. GO TOs are kept under surveillance. Loop indentation and IF...THEN indentation work well together.

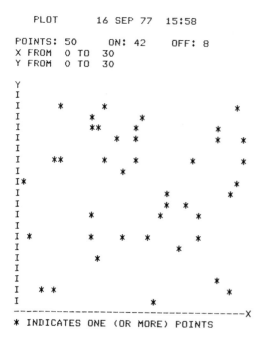

```
     PLOT        16 SEP 77   15:58

POINTS: 50        ON: 42      OFF: 8
X FROM   0 TO   30
Y FROM   0 TO   30
```

* INDICATES ONE (OR MORE) POINTS

```
100 REM     PLOT              17 JULY 1977        JOHN M. NEVISON
110
120 REM     PLOTS ALL POINTS IN THE REGION X1-X2, Y1-Y2. ON PAPER,
130 REM     THE REGION IS W9 CHARACTERS WIDE AND L9 LINES LONG.
140
150 REM     VARIABLES:
160 REM        G()....THE GRAPH MATRIX IN WHICH POINTS ARE MARKED
170 REM        I,J....INDEX VARIABLES
180 REM        O......OUTSIDE POINT COUNTER
190 REM        X,Y....THE COORDINATES OF THE POINT
200
210 REM     CONSTANTS:
220     LET L9 = 20                    'LENGTH OF THE PLOT IN LINES
230     LET N9 = 50                    'NUMBER OF POINTS PLOTTED
240     LET W9 = 36                    'WIDTH OF THE PLOT IN CHARACTERS
250     LET X1 = 0                     'LEFT BOUNDARY OF PLOT
260     LET X2 = 30                    'RIGHT BOUNDARY OF PLOT
270     LET Y1 = 0                     'BOTTOM BOUNDARY OF PLOT
280     LET Y2 = 30                    'TOP BOUNDARY OF PLOT
290
300 REM     DIMENSIONS:
310     DIM G(36,20)
320
330 REM     MAIN PROGRAM
340
350     LET O = 0
360     FOR I = 1 TO L9
370        FOR J = 1 TO W9
380           LET G(J,I) = 0
390        NEXT J
400     NEXT I
410
420     FOR I = 1 TO N9
430        LET X = INT(RND*35 + .5)
440        LET Y = INT(RND*35 + .5)
450        IF X < X1 THEN 550
460         IF X > X2 THEN 550
470          IF Y < Y1 THEN 550
480           IF Y > Y2 THEN 550
490            LET X = X / (X2 - X1)
500            LET Y = Y / (Y2 - Y1)
510            LET X = INT(X*(W9-1) + 1.5)
520            LET Y = INT(Y*(L9-1) + 1.5)
530            LET G(X,Y) = G(X,Y) + 1
540            GOTO 570                 'NEXT I
550
560        LET O = O + 1
570     NEXT I
580
590     PRINT "POINTS:"; N9; "    ON:"; N9-O; "   OFF:"; O
600     PRINT "X FROM "; X1; "TO "; X2
610     PRINT "Y FROM "; Y1; "TO "; Y2
620     PRINT
630     PRINT "Y"
640     FOR I = L9 TO 1 STEP -1
650        PRINT "I";
660        FOR J = 1 TO W9
670           IF G(J,I) <> 0 THEN 700
680           PRINT " ";
690           GO TO 720                 'NEXT J
700
710           PRINT "*";
720        NEXT J
730        PRINT
740     NEXT I
750     FOR J = 1 TO W9+1
760        PRINT "-";
770     NEXT J
780     PRINT "X"
790     PRINT "* INDICATES ONE (OR MORE) POINTS"
800
810     END
```

HISTGRAM is another utility program that can be used in more than one way. Notice how instead of inserting several short lines in the print block, this program makes use of the length function FNL to convert length in units to length in characters across the page.

```
HISTGRAM  16 SEP 77  16:18

FROM 0 TO  3 IN INTERVALS OF  0.15 .
MAXIMUM HEIGHT IS  41 POINTS.
I*
I***
I*
I******
I*********
I*****************
I****************
I******************************
I*********************
I********************************
I***********************************
I**************************
I************************
I****************
I**********
I*****
I**********
I*
I***
I*
```

```
100 REM    HISTGRAM          17 JULY 1977      JOHN M. NEVISON
110
120 REM    PRINT A HISTOGRAM OF THE DISTRIBUTION OF N9 RANDOM NUMBERS.
130
140 REM    VARIABLES:
150 REM       H()...THE LENGTH OF EACH HISTOGRAM BAR
160 REM       I.....THE HISTOGRAM INTERVAL
170 REM       J,K...INDEX VARIABLES
180 REM       M.....THE MAXIMUM H()
190 REM       X.....A RANDOM NUMBER
200
210 REM    CONSTANTS:                       'NUMBER OF HISTOGRAM BARS
220    LET H9 = 20                          'LENGTH OF THE LARGEST BAR
230    LET L9 = 35                          '  IN CHARACTERS ACROSS THE PAGE
240 REM
250    LET N9 = 300                         'NUMBER OF RANDOM NUMBERS
260    LET R9 = 3                           'NUMBER OF RND'S IN EACH X
270
280 REM    DIMENSIONS:
290    DIM H(20)
300
310 REM    FUNCTIONS:
320
330 REM    FNL CONVERTS LENGTH TO LENGTH IN CHARACTERS SO THAT
340 REM    FNL(M) WILL BE L9 CHARACTERS LONG.
350
360    DEF FNL(L) = INT(L/M * (L9-1) + 1.5)
370
380 REM    MAIN PROGRAM
390
400 REM    GENERATE X, SORT IT INTO THE RIGHT HISTOGRAM BAR, H(K),
410 REM    CHECK FOR A NEW MAXIMUM.  WHEN DONE, PRINT THE HISTOGRAM.
420
430    LET I = R9 / H9
440    LET M = 0
450
460    FOR J = 1 TO N9
470
480       LET X = 0
490       FOR K = 1 TO R9
500          LET X = X + RND
510       NEXT K
520
530       LET K = INT(H9*X/R9) + 1
540       LET H(K) = H(K) +1
550       IF H(K) <= M THEN 570
560          LET M = H(K)
570
580    NEXT J
590
600    PRINT "FROM 0 TO "; R9; "IN INTERVALS OF "; I; "."
610    PRINT "MAXIMUM HEIGHT IS "; M; "POINTS."
620    FOR J = 1 TO H9
630       PRINT "I";
640       FOR K = 1 TO FNL(H(J))
650          PRINT "*";
660       NEXT K
670       PRINT
680    NEXT J
690
700    END
```

CARDDEAL is a program with subroutines. Notice how each has a top REM title line and a bottom RETURN. Just after the title line the IN variable list tells what information the program is passing in to the subroutine. The OUT variable list announces what new or altered variables the subroutine is passing out to the program. Constants are available to the whole program. Subroutines allow a program to be broken into one-page pieces, each of which should be easy for the eye to span in a glance.

```
CARDDEAL   16 SEP 77   20:29

QUEEN OF HEARTS     SIX OF SPADES      JACK OF HEARTS     EIGHT OF CLUBS   SIX
  OF CLUBS     FIVE OF HEARTS     TWO OF DIAMONDS     NINE OF SPADES      SEVEN
  OF CLUBS     FIVE OF SPADES     TEN OF HEARTS      TWO OF SPADES      JACK OF
SPADES     TWO OF HEARTS     QUEEN OF DIAMONDS     SIX OF DIAMONDS        THREE
  OF SPADES     THREE OF DIAMONDS     ACE OF HEARTS      KING OF DIAMONDS
KING OF HEARTS     EIGHT OF HEARTS     KING OF SPADES     TWO OF CLUBS
QUEEN OF SPADES     THREE OF CLUBS     TEN OF DIAMONDS     EIGHT OF SPADES
FIVE OF DIAMONDS     FIVE OF CLUBS     THREE OF HEARTS     SEVEN OF SPADES
ACE OF SPADES     ACE OF CLUBS     KING OF CLUBS     SEVEN OF DIAMONDS   NINE
  OF CLUBS     JACK OF DIAMONDS     JACK OF CLUBS     TEN OF CLUBS     FOUR OF
CLUBS     SIX OF HEARTS     TEN OF SPADES     NINE OF HEARTS     FOUR OF
DIAMONDS     QUEEN OF CLUBS     SEVEN OF HEARTS     EIGHT OF DIAMONDS     FOUR
  OF HEARTS     FOUR OF SPADES     ACE OF DIAMONDS     NINE OF DIAMONDS
```

```
100 REM      CARDDEAL       16 SEPTEMBER 1977   JOHN M. NEVISON
105
110 REM      SHUFFLE AND DEAL A DECK OF CARDS, D().
115
120 REM      VARIABLES:
125 REM         C.....THE  PARTICULAR CARD
130 REM         D()...THE DECK OF CARDS
135 REM         I.....INDEX VARIABLE
140 REM         I1....MIXED INDEX VARIABLE
145 REM         R.....THE RANK NUMBER (1-13)
150 REM         R$....THE RANK OF CARD
155 REM         S.....THE SUIT NUMBER (1-4)
160 REM         S$....THE SUIT OF THE CARD
165 REM         X.....THE EXCHANGE VARIABLE
170
175 REM      CONSTANT:                      'NUMBER OF CARDS IN THE DECK
180     LET N9 = 52
185
190 REM      DIMENSIONS:
195     DIM D(52)
200
205 REM      FUNCTIONS:
210 REM       FIND THE RANK NUMBER OF THE CARD(1-13)
215     DEF FNR(C) = C - 13*INT((C-1)/13)
220
225 REM       FIND THE SUIT NUMBER OF THE CARD(1-4)
230     DEF FNS(C) = INT((C-1)/13) + 1
235
237
240 REM      MAIN ROUTINE
245
250     FOR I = 1 TO N9
255        LET D(I) = I
260     NEXT I
265
270     GO SUB 325                      'SHUFFLE
275
280     FOR I = 1 TO N9
285        LET C = D(I)
290        GO SUB  420                  ' FIND RANK OF CARD
295        GO SUB  755                  ' FIND SUIT OF CARD
300        PRINT R$; " OF "; S$; "     ";
305     NEXT I
310
315     STOP
320
322
325 REM      SUBROUTINE:  SHUFFLE
330 REM        IN:  D()
335 REM        OUT: D()
340
345 REM      SHUFFLE THE DECK BY PICKING ONE CARD AT A TIME
350 REM      AND MOVING IT TO THE SIDE.
355
360     LET I1 = 0
365     LET X = 0
370
375     FOR I = N9 TO 1 STEP -1
380        LET I1 = INT(RND*I + 1)
385        LET X = D(I1)
390        LET D(I1) = D(I)
395        LET D(I) = X
400     NEXT I
405
410 RETURN
415
```

```
420 REM      SUBROUTINE; FIND RANK OF CARD
425 REM        IN:  C
430 REM        OUT:  R$
435
440 REM        FIND THE RANK, K, AND  GO TO THE RIGHT NAME.
450
455      LET R =  FNR(C)
460
465      IF R > 7 THEN 475
470        ON R GO TO 485,505, 525, 545, 565, 585, 605
475        ON K-7 GO TO 625, 645, 665, 685, 705, 725
480
485 REM     1 ACE
490      LET R$ = "ACE"
495      GO TO 740                          ' ON BOTTOM
500
505 REM     2 TWO
510      LET R$ = "TWO"
515      GO TO 740                          'ON BOTTOM
520
525 REM     3 THREE
530      LET R$ = "THREE"
535      GO TO 740                          ' ON BOTTOM
540
545 REM     4 FOUR
550      LET R$ = "FOUR"
555      GO TO 740                          'ON BOTTOM
560
565 REM     5 FIVE
570      LET R$ = "FIVE"
575      GO TO 740                          'ON BOTTOM
580
585 REM     6 SIX
590      LET R$ = "SIX"
595      GO TO 740                          'ON BOTTOM
600
605 REM     7 SEVEN
610      LET R$ = "SEVEN"
615      GO TO 740                          'ON BOTTOM
620
625 REM     8 EIGHT
630      LET R$ = "EIGHT"
635      GO TO 740                          'ON BOTTOM
640
645 REM     9 NINE
650      LET R$ = "NINE"
655      GO TO 740                          'ON BOTTOM
660
665 REM     10 TEN
670      LET R$ = "TEN"
675      GO TO 740                          'ON BOTTOM
680
685 REM     11 JACK
690      LET R$ = "JACK"
695      GO TO 740                          'ON BOTTOM
700
705 REM     12 QUEEN
710      LET R$ = "QUEEN"
715      GO TO 740                          'ON BOTTOM
720
725 REM     13 KING
730      LET R$ = "KING"
735      GO TO 740                          'ON BOTTOM
740
745 RETURN
750
```

```
755 REM      SUBROUTINE:  FIND SUIT OF CARD
760 REM        IN:  C
765 REM       OUT:  S$
770
775 REM       FIND THE SUIT, S, AND GO TO THE RIGHT NAME.
780
785     LET S = FNS(C)
790
795     ON S GO TO 805, 825, 845, 865
800
805 REM    1 CLUBS
810     LET S$ = "CLUBS"
815     GO TO 880                         'ON BOTTOM
820
825 REM    2 DIAMONDS
830     LET S$ = "DIAMONDS"
835     GO TO 880                         'ON BOTTOM
840
845 REM    3 HEARTS
850     LET S$ = "HEARTS"
855     GO TO 880                         'ON BOTTOM
860
865 REM    4 SPADES
870     LET S$ = "SPADES"
875     GO TO 880                         ' ON BOTTOM
880
885 RETURN
890
895     END
```

7-SUM is a two-page program with subroutines. It illustrates how these subroutines can be kept under control. Constants are collected at the head of the program, but variables are initialized where they are first used. Detailed explanations occur near the code they explain.

```
7-SUM      16 SEP 77  16:25

HEIGHTS OF THE HIGHEST POINT IN 50 STATES
UNIT--(100 FEET)

NUMBER OF DATA: 50

                DEPTH  MID      RAW SUMMARY            SPREAD
                ---------------------------------------------------------------------
MEDIAN          25.5   46    I       46           I
HINGE(QTR)      13     46    I  20          112    I   92
EIGHTH          7      61    I  13          135    I   122
EXTREMES        1      100   I  3           203    I   200




7-SUM      16 SEP 77  16:28

HEIGHTS OF THE HIGHEST POINT IN 50 STATES
UNIT--(100 FEET)

NUMBER OF DATA: 50

                DEPTH  MID       ROOT SUMMARY          SPREAD
                ---------------------------------------------------------------------
MEDIAN          25.5   6.78073 I      6.78073        I
HINGE(QTR)      13     3.05543 I  4.47214    10.583  I   6.11087
EIGHTH          7      4.0067  I  3.60555    11.619  I   8.0134
EXTREMES        1      6.25788 I  1.73205    14.2478 I   12.5158
```

```
100 REM     7-SUM                17 JULY 1977      JOHN M. NEVISON
105
110 REM     FIND THE 7-NUMBER SUMMARY OF A BATCH OF NUMBERS.
115 REM     (BY VARYING THE FUNCTION FNF(X) ON SUCCESIVE RUNS
120 REM     ONE CAN FIND AN EXPRESSION THAT LINES UP MID-SPREADS.)
125 REM     FUNCTIONS TO TRY INCLUDE:
130 REM     X^2, X, X^(1/2), LOG(X), -X^(-1/2), -X^(-1), -X^(-2)
135
140 REM     REFERENCE:  JOHN W. TUKEY, "EXPLORATORY DATA ANALYSIS,"
145 REM                 READING, MASS.:  ADDISON-WESLEY PUBLISHING
150 REM                 COMPANY, 1977.
155
160 REM     VARIABLES:
165 REM         B()...THE BATCH OF NUMBERS (SORTED)
170 REM         D()...THE DEPTH OF THE LETTER VALUES
175 REM         I.....INDEX VARIABLE
180 REM         S()...SUMMARY VALUES
185
190 REM     CONSTANTS:                       'NUMBER OF DATA
195     LET N9 = 50                          'NUMBER OF SUMMARY VALUES =
200     LET S9 = 3                           '   2*S9 + 1
205 REM
210     LET T$ = "RAW"                       'TITLE FOR DISPLAY (VARIES
215 REM                                      '   WITH FNF)
220
225 REM     DIMENSIONS:
230     DIM B(50)
235
240
245 REM     FUNCTIONS:
250     DEF FNF(X) =  X
255
260 REM     MAIN PROGRAM
265
270     FOR I = 1 TO N9
275         READ B(I)
280         LET B(I) = FNF(B(I))
285     NEXT I
290     DATA 3,4,5,8,8,12,13,16,17,18,18,20,20,23,24,24,28
295     DATA 32,34,35,35,36,40,41,44,48,49,50,53,53,54,57
300     DATA 63,66,67,72,88,112,126,127,128,131,132,135,138,138
305     DATA 144,144,145,203
310
315     GO SUB 340                           'DEPTHS AND SUMMARY VALUES
320     GO SUB 515                           'PRINT OUT
325
330     STOP
335
```

```
340 REM     SUBROUTINE:  DEPTHS AND SUMMARY VALUES
345 REM       IN:  B()
350 REM       OUT:  D(),S()
355
360 REM     DEPTHS ARE THE DISTANCE TO THE NEAREST END OF THE
365 REM     ORDERED DATA.   THEY ARE EITHER A WHOLE NUMBER OR A NUMBER
370 REM     AND A HALF.   QUARTERS AND EIGHTHS, LIKE THE MEDIAN, ARE
375 REM     EITHER NUMBERS IN THE ROW (WHEN DEPTH IS A WHOLE NUMBER),
380 REM     OR THE AVERAGE OF TWO ADJACENT VALUES.
385
390     FOR I = 1 TO 2*S9 + 1
395        LET D(I) = 0
400        LET S(I) = 0
405     NEXT I
410
415     LET D(0) = N9
420     FOR I = 1 TO S9
425        LET D(I) = (INT(D(I-1)) + 1) / 2
430     NEXT I
435
440     FOR I = 1 TO S9
445        IF D(I) <> INT(D(I)) THEN 465
450        LET S(I) = B(D(I))
455        LET S(I+S9) = B((N9+1) - D(I))
460        GO TO 485                       'NEXT I
465
470        LET D = INT(D(I))
475        LET S(I) = (B(D) + B(D+1)) / 2
480        LET S(I+S9) = (B(N9+1-D) + B(N9-D)) / 2
485     NEXT I
490
495 RETURN
500
505 REM     SUBROUTINE:  PRINT OUT
510 REM       IN:  B(), D(), L()
515 REM       OUT:
520
525     PRINT "HEIGHTS OF THE HIGHEST POINT IN 50 STATES"
530     PRINT "UNIT--(100 FEET)"
535     PRINT
540     PRINT "NUMBER OF DATA:"; N9
545     PRINT
550     PRINT TAB(11); "DEPTH"; TAB(18); "MID";
555     PRINT TAB(29); T$; " SUMMARY"; TAB(51); "SPREAD"
560     PRINT TAB(18); "------------------------------------------"
565     PRINT "MEDIAN    "; D(1); TAB(17); S(1);
570     PRINT TAB(26); "I"; TAB(32); S(1); TAB(48); "I"
575
580     PRINT "HINGE(QTR)"; D(2); TAB(17); (S(2+S9) - S(2)) / 2;
585     PRINT TAB(26); "I"; TAB(28); S(2); TAB(38);S(2+S9);
590     PRINT TAB(48); "I"; TAB(50); S(2+S9)-S(2)
595
600     PRINT "EIGHTH    "; D(3); TAB(17); (S(3+S9) - S(3)) / 2;
605     PRINT TAB(26); "I"; TAB(28); S(3); TAB(38); S(3+S9);
610     PRINT TAB(48); "I"; TAB(50); S(3+S9) - S(3)
615
620     PRINT "EXTREMES  "; 1; TAB(17); (B(N9) - B(1)) / 2;
625     PRINT TAB(26); "I"; TAB(28); B(1); TAB(38); B(N9);
630     PRINT TAB(48); "I"; TAB(50); B(N9)-B(1)
635
640 RETURN
645
650     END
```

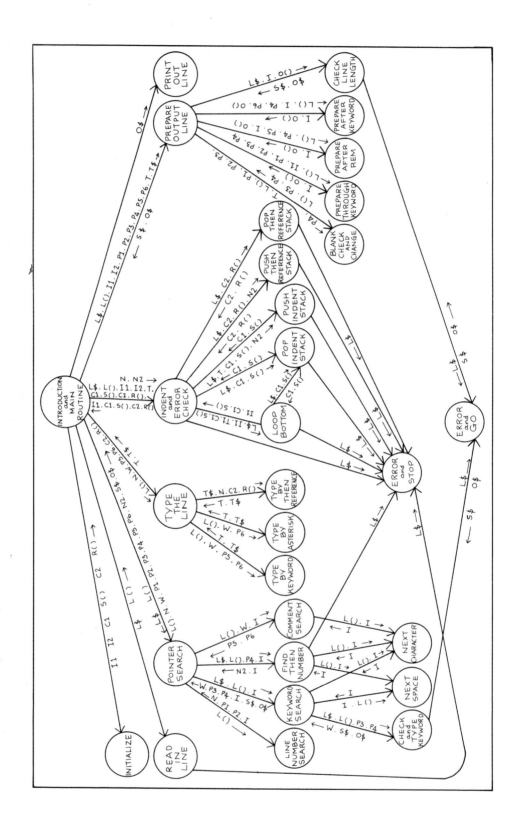

BEYOND
BASIC:
LARGER
PROGRAMS

6

Though this be madness, yet there is method in it.

WILLIAM SHAKESPEARE
Hamlet

In general, writing a large program consists of systematically writing many small ones. Working on a large program requires that everything be performed top-down, one level at a time. Write top-down: comment top-down, code top-down, type top-down, practice top-down. As you write a large program, the rules of style must be scrupulously observed at each step.

The reader who goes over this chapter carefully is probably about to step outside the bounds of this book and into a Basic program longer than one page. Anyone who takes this proud step should first learn something about structured programming, about forms like IF...THEN...ELSE, DO...WHILE, REPEAT...UNTIL, and CASE, and about how to compose a program a piece at a time from the top down. After becoming familiar with these ideas you should be prepared to impose strict standards of style on the program to compensate for the lack of controls in Basic.

The most important standard to enforce is that each piece of the program should be less than one page long. The piece's size is governed by two needs: easy reading and coherent function. One page should be the upper limit for most pieces because it guarantees that the reader will not have to flip back and forth between pages to see how the code works. Everything on a single page means everything under visual control.

Coherent function, however, has its demands. Things that do something together should be grouped together. The more coherent a program's pieces are, the fewer the variables that must be passed back and forth. The fewer the variables, the more limited the pathways for the error and the more likely the error will remain trapped in its own piece.

In Minimal Basic each piece after the main program is a subroutine. The program gets to a subroutine from a GO SUB statement and goes back to where

it left the main program when it comes to a RETURN statement. The tag on a
GO SUB should show the name of the subroutine exactly as it appears in the
title line of the subroutine. The RETURN statement should be easy to see so the
reader knows where one subroutine ends and the next begins.

Like any good block of program, each subroutine should begin at the top
and end at the bottom. If the program sometimes finishes its work in the middle
of a piece, it should go to the bottom to exit. There should be only one RETURN
for each subroutine.

When a coherent subroutine runs over one page, its size usually can be
reduced by spawning new subroutines from the parent. Each new subroutine
should strive for its own internal cohesion, take only those variables it needs
from its parent, and return to the parent only those variables that the parent
requires. The program that follows, STYLIST, is a large program written in
Minimal Basic. Because large programs demand good structure and very few
devices to ensure good structure exist in Minimal Basic, it is not a good idea to
write large programs in this limited language. However, if you attempt a large
program with a limited language, you should use *every available device* to
structure the code as much as possible. STYLIST shows what can be done with
the primitive tools of Minimal Basic by scrupulously observing the rules of style.

If your Basic has string functions and subscripted string variables, you
should be able to write a program that is much shorter and easier to understand
than STYLIST. One big change would be a GET NEXT WORD subroutine.

STYLIST itself is a software tool, a program that uses another program as
data. As the introduction will explain, STYLIST cleans up a program according
to Rules 3, 18, and 19. You may view this program as a rephrasing of these
rules, not in English, but in Minimal Basic. STYLIST *does* what the rules talked
about doing. So STYLIST itself is a second way to communicate the ideas
discussed earlier.

STYLIST is also its own example. It was run on a copy of itself, and the
result replaced the original. The twenty-nine subroutines of STYLIST all exhibit
the rules of style in a working program.

```
1000 REM     STYLIST              11 MAY 1977        JOHN M. NEVISON
1005 REM                                             JOHN M. NEVISON ASSOC.
1010 REM                                             3   SPRUCE STREET
1015 REM                                             BOSTON, MA   02108
1020 REM                                             (617) 227 2889
1025
1030 REM     STYLIST INDENTS STRUCTURES IN A MINIMAL BASIC
1035 REM     PROGRAM ACCORDING TO THE SUGGESTIONS IN RULE 16
1037 REM     OF 'THE LITTLE BOOK OF BASIC STYLE.'  LOOPS ARE
1038 REM     INDENTED 3 SPACES.  (SEE CONSTANT I8.)   LINES
1039 REM     BENEATH AN IF...THEN ARE INDENTED 1 SPACE.
1040 REM     (SEE CONSTANT I9.)
1050
```

```
1055 REM    STYLIST ADOPTS THE REM-5 CONVENTION OF RULE 3.
1060 REM    CODE IS INDENTED AT LEAST 5 SPACES. (SEE CONSTANT I7.)
1065 REM    REM'S ARE INDENTED ONE SPACE AND THE COMMENT
1070 REM    IS TABBED OVER AT LEAST 4 SPACES. (SEE CONSTANT R9.)
1075
1080 REM    RETURN'S ARE  INDENTED ONLY ONE SPACE TO MARK THE
1085 REM    THE END OF A SUBROUTINE CLEARLY.
1086
1087 REM    NOTE***.   STYLIST IS WRITTEN IN MINIMAL BASIC.
1088 REM    MINIMAL BASIC DOES NOT HANDLE STRINGS OF CHARACTERS
1089 REM    WELL.  IF YOUR BASIC HAS ADDITIONAL STRING FUNCTIONS
1090 REM    SUCH AS 'CHANGE', YOU CAN DESIGN A BETTER PROGRAM.
1091
1095 REM    REFERENCE:   JOHN M. NEVISON, "THE LITTLE BOOK OF
1100 REM                 BASIC STYLE," READING,MASS.:   ADDISON-
1105 REM                 WESLEY PUBLISHING COMPANY,1978.
1110
1115 REM    STYLIST WILL PRODUCE EITHER REGULAR BLANK LINES OR PSEUDO
1120 REM    BLANK REM LINES. (SEE THE CONSTANT B9).
1125
1130 REM    STYLIST MOVES ON-LINE COMMENTS OVER TO THE RIGHT. (SEE
1135 REM    THE CONSTANT C9).
1140
1145 REM    STYLIST NEVER ADDS OR SUBTRACTS A LINE FROM
1150 REM    THE INPUT PROGRAM.
1155
1160 REM    STYLIST STYLED ITSELF.  THIS PROGRAM'S FORMAT IS THE
1165 REM    RESULT OF A RUN OF THE CURRENT PROGRAM ON ITSELF.  ITS
1170 REM    FORM DOCUMENTS ITS CONTENT.
1175
1180 REM    LIMITATIONS:
1185
1190 REM    THE INPUT PROGRAM MUST MEET CERTAIN REQUIREMENTS:
1195
1200 REM        1. IT MUST ALREADY HAVE *RUN* SUCCESSFULLY.
1205
1210 REM        2. EVERY KEYWORD MUST HAVE A BLANK SPACE BEFORE AND
1215 REM        AFTER.
1220
1225 REM        3. AN ON-LINE COMMENT OR A REM ON-LINE COMMENT MUST
1230 REM        BEGIN WITH AN APOSTROPHE('). TO USE A DIFFERENT SYMBOL,
1235 REM        CHANGE THE CONSTANT A9.
1240
1245 REM        4. GO TO LOOPS MUST BE MARKED WITH AN APOSTROPHE
1250 REM        ASTERISK('*) ON THE FIRST LINE AND ON THE GOTO LINE.
1255 REM        (SEE THE MAIN LOOP OF THIS PROGRAM FOR AN EXAMPLE).
1260
1265 REM    THIS PROGRAM USES BLANK LINES AND ON-LINE COMMENTS IN
1270 REM    EXCEPTION TO THE MINIMAL BASIC STANDARD.  ANY OTHER
1275 REM    EXCEPTIONS ARE MARKED  'NOT MINIMAL BASIC ***
1280 REM    AND EXPLAINED IN NEARBY REMARKS.  EXCEPTIONS ARE LIMITED TO
1285 REM    FOUR PLACES:  THE INTRODUCTION, READ IN LINE,
1290 REM    CHECK LINE LENGTH, AND PRINT OUT LINE.
1295
1300 REM    THE FUNCTION THAT COMPUTES THE LINE NUMBERS, FNN(A),
1305 REM    DEPENDS ON THE CHARACTERS FOR NUMBERS BEGINNING
1310 REM    WITH 0 IN A(48) AND ASCENDING CONSECUTIVELY THROUGH A(57).
1315 REM    OTHER CHARACTER SETS WHERE THE NUMERALS ARE NOT TOGETHER
1320 REM    AND IN ORDER WILL REQUIRE A DIFFERENT FUNCTION.
1325
```

```
1330 REM      ORGANIZATION:
1335
1340 REM      SUBROUTINE CALLS (* MEANS NOT THE FIRST OCCURRENCE)
1345 REM      I. INTRODUCTION
1350 REM      II.MAIN ROUTINE
1355 REM         INITIALIZE
1360 REM         READ IN LINE
1365 REM            ERROR AND STOP
1370 REM         POINTER SEARCH
1375 REM            LINE NUMBER SEARCH
1380 REM            KEYWORD SEARCH
1385 REM               NEXT CHARACTER
1390 REM               NEXT SPACE
1395 REM               CHECK AND TYPE KEYWORD
1400 REM                  ERROR AND GO
1405 REM            FIND THEN NUMBER
1410 REM               NEXT SPACE *
1415 REM               NEXT CHARACTER *
1420 REM               ERROR AND STOP *
1425 REM            COMMENT SEARCH
1430 REM               NEXT CHARACTER *
1435 REM         TYPE THE LINE
1440 REM            TYPE BY KEYWORD
1445 REM            TYPE BY ASTERISK
1450 REM            TYPE BY THEN REFERENCE
1455 REM         INDENT AND ERROR CHECK
1460 REM            PUSH INDENT STACK
1465 REM               ERROR AND STOP *
1470 REM            LOOP BOTTOM
1475 REM               POP INDENT STACK
1480 REM                  ERROR AND STOP *
1485 REM               ERROR AND STOP *
1490 REM            PUSH THEN REFERENCE STACK
1495 REM            ERROR AND STOP *
1500 REM            POP INDENT STACK *
1505 REM            POP THEN REFERENCE STACK
1510 REM         PREPARE OUTPUT LINE
1515 REM            BLANK CHECK AND CHANGE
1520 REM            PREPARE THROUGH KEYWORD
1525 REM            PREPARE AFTER KEYWORD
1530 REM            PREPARE AFTER REM
1535 REM            CHECK LINE LENGTH
1540 REM               ERROR AND GO *
1545 REM         PRINT OUT LINE
1550
1555 REM      FOR A DISCUSSION OF LEGAL MINIMAL BASIC CHARACTERS AND
1560 REM      KEYWORDS, SEE:
1565 REM         AMERICAN NATIONAL STANDARDS INSTITUTE,
1570 REM         "MINIMAL BASIC," PUBLICATION NUMBER X3.60, 1430
1575 REM         BROADWAY, NEW YORK, NY 10018, 1977.
1580
1585 REM      CONSTANTS:
1590
1595      DIM A(127)
1600      FOR I = 1 TO 127
1605         READ A(I)                        'THE LEGAL ASCII CHARACTER CODE
1610      NEXT I
1615      DATA 0,0,0,0,0,0,0,0,0,0
1620      DATA 0,0,0,0,0,0,0,0,0,0
1625      DATA 0,0,0,0,0,0,0,0,0,0
1630 REM           SP    !    "    #    $    %    &    '    (
1635      DATA  0, 32, 33, 34, 35, 36, 37, 38, 39, 40
1640 REM       )    *    +    ,    -    .    /    0    1    2
1645      DATA 41, 42, 43, 44, 45, 46, 47, 48, 49, 50
```

```
1650 REM         3    4    5    6    7    8    9    :    ;    <
1655      DATA 51, 52, 53, 54, 55, 56, 57, 58, 59, 60
1660 REM         =    >    ?         A    B    C    D    E    F
1665      DATA 61, 62, 63,  0, 65, 66, 67, 68, 69, 70
1670 REM         G    H    I    J    K    L    M    N    O    P
1675      DATA 71, 72, 73, 74, 75, 76, 77, 78, 79, 80
1680 REM         Q    R    S    T    U    V    W    X    Y    Z
1685      DATA 81, 82, 83, 84, 85, 86, 87, 88, 89, 90
1690 REM                        ^    _
1695      DATA 0, 0, 0, 94, 95, 0, 0, 0, 0, 0
1700      DATA 0,0,0,0,0,0,0,0,0,0
1705      DATA 0,0,0,0,0,0,0,0,0,0
1710      DATA 0,0,0,0,0,0,0
1715
1720 REM     FOUR OF THE FOLOWING KEYWORDS ARE NOT USED IN THIS
1725 REM     PROGRAM BECAUSE THEY ARE NOT THE *FIRST*
1730 REM     KEYWORD ON THE LINE.  A REVISION OF THIS PROGRAM
1735 REM     MIGHT WANT TO CHECK FOR *ALL* THE MINIMAL BASIC
1740 REM     WORDS AND SO THEY ARE INCLUDED HERE.
1745 REM     THE WORDS NOT USED ARE:  STEP, SUB, THEN,
1750 REM     AND TO.
1755
1760      LET K9 = 26                       'NUMBER OF KEYWORDS
1765      DIM W(26,10)
1770      FOR I = 1 TO K9
1775         READ W(I,0)
1780         FOR J = 1 TO W(I,0)
1785            READ W(I,J)                  'LEGAL MINIMAL BASIC KEYWORDS
1790         NEXT J
1795      NEXT I
1800
1805 REM     0-BLANK
1810 REM     1-BASE
1815      DATA 4, 66, 65, 83, 69
1820 REM     2-DATA
1825      DATA 4, 68, 65, 84, 65
1830 REM     3-DEF
1835      DATA 3, 68, 69, 70
1840 REM     4-DIM
1845      DATA 3, 68, 73, 77
1850 REM     5-END
1855      DATA 3, 69, 78, 68
1860 REM     6-FOR
1865      DATA 3, 70, 79, 82
1870 REM     7-GO
1875      DATA 2, 71, 79
1880 REM     8-GOSUB
1885      DATA 5, 71, 79, 83, 85, 66
1890 REM     9-GOTO
1895      DATA 4, 71, 79, 84, 79
1900 REM     10-IF
1905      DATA 2, 73, 70
1910 REM     11-INPUT
1915      DATA 5, 73, 78, 80, 85, 84
1920 REM     12-LET
1925      DATA 3, 76, 69, 84
1930 REM     13-NEXT
1935      DATA 4, 78, 69, 88, 84
1940 REM     14-ON
1945      DATA 2, 79, 78
1950 REM     15-OPTION
1955      DATA 6, 79, 80, 84, 73, 79, 78
1960 REM     16-PRINT
1965      DATA 5, 80, 82, 73, 78, 84
```

```
1970 REM      17-RANDOMIZE
1975      DATA 9, 82, 65, 78, 68, 79, 77, 73, 90, 69
1980 REM      18-READ
1985      DATA 4, 82, 69, 65, 68
1990 REM      19-REM
1995      DATA 3, 82, 69, 77
2000 REM      20-RESTORE
2005      DATA 7, 82, 69, 83, 84, 79, 82, 69
2010 REM      21-RETURN
2015      DATA 6, 82, 69, 84, 85, 82, 78
2020 REM      22-STEP
2025      DATA 4, 83, 84, 69, 80
2030 REM      23-STOP
2035      DATA 4, 83, 84, 79, 80
2040 REM      24-SUB
2045      DATA 3, 83, 85, 66
2050 REM      25-THEN
2055      DATA 4, 84, 72, 69, 78
2060 REM      26-TO
2065      DATA 2, 84, 79
2070
2075      LET A9 = A(39)               'THE CHARACTER THAT BEGINS AN
2080 REM                               '   ON-LINE COMMENT
2085      LET B9 = 1                   'BLANK SWITCH--
2090 REM                               '   1 = BLANK, 0 = REM BLANK
2095      LET C9 = 40                  'ON LINE COMMENT POSITION
2100      LET D9 = 20                  'DEPTH OF STACKS, S() AND R().
2105      LET E9 = 48                  'LENGTH OF EXCESS OUTPUT LINE
2110 REM                               '   ROUGHLY EQUAL TO L9-W9 +INDENT
2115      LET I7 = 5                   'MINIMUM CODE INDENTATION
2120      LET I8 = 3                   'LOOP INDENTATION
2125      LET I9 = 1                   'IF...THEN INDENTATION
2130 REM      K9                       'NUMBER OF KEYWORDS(ABOVE)
2135      LET L9 = 100                 'LENGTH OF L()
2140      LET M9 = 1E25                'A VERY LARGE NUMBER
2145      LET O9 = 100                 'LENGTH OF O()
2150      LET R9 = 4                   'MINIMUM REM TAB
2155      LET W9 = 72                  'MAXIMUM WIDTH OF OUTPUT LINE
2160
2165 REM      DIMENSIONS:
2170
2175      DIM L(100),O(100)
2180      DIM S(20,2), R(20)
2185      DIM E(48)
2190
2195 REM      VARIABLES:
2200 REM          C1......COUNTER FOR INDENT STACK S()
2205 REM          C2......COUNTER FOR THEN REFERENCE STACK R()
2210 REM          E().....EXCESS LINE VECTOR--PART EXCEEDING W9 CHARS
2215 REM          E$......EXCESS LINE STRING
2220 REM          I1......THE INDENT OF THE LINE
2225 REM          I2......THE INDENT OF THE PREVIOUS LINE
2230 REM          I3......A TEMPORARY STORAGE FOR I1
2235 REM          H,I,J,K.INDEX VARIABLES
2240 REM          L().....THE LINE AS A VECTOR OF DECIMAL CODE FOR
2245 REM          L$......THE LINE OF THE INPUT PROGRAM
2250 REM                  THE ASCII CHARACTERS.
2255 REM          N.......THE LINE NUMBER
2260 REM          N2......THE THEN REFERENCE--ANOTHER LINE NUMBER
2265 REM          O().....THE OUTPUT LINE VECTOR
2270 REM          O$......THE OUTPUT LINE
2275 REM          P1,P2...POINTER TO BEGINNING AND END OF LINE NUMBER.
2280 REM          P3,P4,..POINTER TO BEGINNING AND END OF KEYWORD.
2285 REM          P5......POINTER TO BEGINNING OF REM'S COMMENT
2290 REM          P6......POINTER TO ON-LINE COMMENT (APOSTROPHE)
2295 REM          Q.......THE QUOTATION MARK COUNTER
```

```
2300 REM          R().....THEN REFERENCE STACK
2305 REM          S().....INDENT STACK
2310 REM          S$......SKIP THE LINE FLAG
2315 REM          T.......THE TYPE OF LINE BY NUMBER
2320 REM          T1......THE PROPER TYPE OF TOP LINE FOR A LOOP
2325 REM          T$......THE TYPE OF LINE BY NAME
2330 REM          W.......THE KEYWORD TYPE
2335
2340 REM     FUNCTIONS:
2345
2350 REM     FNN RETURNS THE VALUE OF THE ASCII NUMERAL, A.
2355
2360      DEF FNN(A) = A - A(48)
2365
2370 REM     FILES:
2375
2380 REM     THE FILE AND SCRATCH STATEMENTS DECLARE THE
2385 REM     NAMES OF THE FILES AND CLEAR THE SECOND ONE FOR OUTPUT.
2390 REM     FILE NUMBER ONE IS THE PROGRAM TO BE STYLED.
2395
2400      FILE #1: "INPUT"              'NOT MINIMAL BASIC ***
2405      FILE #2: "OUTPUT"             'NOT MINIMAL BASIC ***
2410      SCRATCH #2                    'NOT MINIMAL BASIC ***
2415
2420 REM     -------------------------------------------------------
2425
2430
```

The introduction to this program is large because the program itself is large. The reference to the book that can provide further documentation appears early in the text. Limitations are discussed. A variable list, alphabetized for quick reference, is included. The constants are labeled. Most of the constants are written in a similar form (I9, B9, etc.) for easy recognition. All the ASCII characters are parameterized so the program can be altered to work on a system with an unstandard character code. The on-line comment character, A9, is a constant labeled by another constant. By putting in the second level, the program can be changed to recognize some character other than an apostrophe (') as the on-line comment character. When working with a large program, parameterize everything.

An outline of the program's subroutine calls is included in the introduction. This gives the reader a concise overview of the entire program and how it works. An additional aid to understanding a large program is a *structure chart* such as the one in the illustration opposite the opening of this chapter. The chart is not a flow chart: it focuses attention not on the flow of control, but on the invocation of subroutines. It shows which routines call which others and what variables are used by the subroutine (IN) and what variables may be altered by the subroutine (OUT). Constructing such a chart should be a part of the initial design of the program. Like comment, it should be sharpened and refined along with new developments in the code, and a final copy should be a part of any documentation that describes the completed program. The outline of subroutine calls should agree with the structure chart.

```
2435 REM       MAIN ROUTINE
2440
2445 REM       FIRST INITIALIZE THE THE PROGRAM-WIDE VARIABLES.
2450 REM       READ A LINE, WORK ON IT, AND PRINT IT OUT--UNTIL THE
2455 REM       KEYWORD IS END (W = 5).
2460
2465 REM       THE LINE IS TYPED BY 'TYPE THE LINE' WITH THE
2470 REM       FOLLOWING VALUES FOR T AND T$:
2475
2480 REM       1-BLANK         5-RETURN    9-NEXT          13-THEN REM O-L
2485 REM       2-REM BLANK     6-'* GOTO    10-IF...THEN    14-THEN STUFF
2490 REM       3-REM ON-LINE   7-'* TOP     11-THEN BLANK   15-OTHER
2495 REM       4-REM           8-FOR        12-THEN REM BLANK
2500
2505 REM       TYPES 1-4 ARE NECESSARY WHEN PREPARING THE LINE FOR OUTPUT
2510 REM       WITH THE REM-5 CONVENTION AND ON-LINE COMMENTS.  TYPES 6-14
2515 REM       ARE USED TO DEFINE AND INDENT STRUCTURES.  TYPES 11-14
2520 REM       ARE LATER USED TO PREPARE THE LINE FOR OUTPUT.
2525
2530           GO SUB 2630                       'INITIALIZE
2535           LET S$ = "OKAY"                   '*
2540             GO SUB 2730                     'READ IN LINE
2545             GO SUB 2915                     'POINTER SEARCH
2550           IF S$ = "SKIP LINE" THEN 2595
2555             GO SUB 4180                     'TYPE THE LINE
2560             IF T < 6 THEN 2575
2565              IF T = 15 THEN 2575
2570               GO SUB 4785                   'INDENT AND ERROR CHECK
2575
2580             GOSUB 5640                      'PREPARE OUTPUT LINE
2585             IF S$ = "SKIP LINE" THEN 2595
2590               LET I2 = I1
2595
2600             GO SUB 6870                     'PRINT OUT LINE
2605             IF W = 5 THEN 2615
2610           GO TO 2535                        '*
2615
2620           STOP
2625
```

The main routine is remarkably small. The secret of its small size is that it delegates most work to subroutines. Each GO SUB statement is tagged with the exact name of the subroutine so that just by reading the tags you can begin to understand how the program works. The downward flow of the program is not broken when there is an error. When S$ = "SKIP LINE" the program goes *down* the page.

```
2630 REM     SUBROUTINE: INITIALIZE
2635 REM       IN:
2640 REM     OUT:   I1, I2, C1, S(), C2, R()
2645
2650 REM     INITIALIZE ALL PROGRAM-WIDE VARIABLES
2655
2660       LET C1 = 0
2665       LET C2 = 0
2670       FOR I = 0 TO D9
2675         LET S(I,1) = 0
2680         LET S(I,2) = 0
2685         LET R(I) = 0
2690       NEXT I
2695
2700       LET R(0) = M9
2705       LET I1 = I7
2710       LET I2 = I7
2715
2720 RETURN
2725
```

Every single variable, with the exception of FOR indices, is initialized before it is used. Variables that will appear outside the main loop must be initialized before the program begins the main loop. All other variables are left to their respective subroutines.

Below the subroutine title, the line marked IN reveals that no variables were passed in to this subroutine. The line marked OUT shows that six variables were altered here and passed out to the main program. The reason for listing the variables that come in or go out is to help track errors. It also prepares the writer to use a powerful feature not found in Minimal Basic, but available in some other versions: a subroutine call which passes only specific variables. Such a feature makes it possible to limit automatically the information passed between subroutines. By marking down what variables passed in and out of a subroutine, you can cultivate the habit of keeping an eye on the information flow.

```
2730 REM     SUBROUTINE:  READ IN LINE
2735 REM       IN:
2740 REM     OUT: L$, L()
2745
2750 REM     THE LINPUT AND CHANGE STATEMENTS ARE NOT MINIMAL BASIC.
2755 REM     LINPUT INPUTS A WHOLE LINE, L$.   THE CHANGE STATEMENT
2760 REM     PRODUCES A ROW VECTOR OF NUMBERS WHICH ARE THE
2765 REM     DECIMAL CODE FOR THE  ASCII CHARACTERS.
2770 REM     THE FIRST ENTRY, L(0), CONTAINS THE LENGTH
2775 REM     OF THE VECTOR.  IF L$ = "THE LINE" THE L VECTOR WOULD BE:
2780 REM         L(0) L(1) L(2) L(3) L(4) L(5) L(6) L(7) L(8)
2785 REM          8    84   72   69   32   76   73   78   69
2790
2795 REM     DIFFERENT SYSTEMS WILL BE FORCED TO IMPLEMENT THIS
2800 REM     SUBROUTINE IN DIFFERENT WAYS.  MICRO-COMPUTERS
2805 REM     MAY WANT TO HAVE AN EXTRA PIECE OF MACHINE LANGUAGE
2810 REM     TO PERFORM THIS SUBROUTINE.
2815
```

```
2820 REM      DETAILS ON THESE STATEMENTS CAN BE FOUND IN:
2825 REM          STEPHEN V.F.WAITE AND DIANE G. MATHER, EDS.
2830 REM          "BASIC, SIXTH EDITION," HANOVER, NH:  UNIVERSITY
2835 REM          PRESS OF NEW ENGLAND, 1971.
2840
2845     LET L$ = " "
2850     FOR I = 0 TO L9
2855        LET L(I) = 0
2860     NEXT I
2865
2870     IF MORE #1 THEN 2885           'NOT MINIMAL BASIC ***
2875       PRINT "INPUT FILE IS OUT OF DATA."
2880       GO SUB 6820                   'ERROR AND STOP
2885
2890     LINPUT #1: L$                  'NOT MINIMAL BASIC ***
2895     CHANGE L$ TO L                 'NOT MINIMAL BASIC ***
2900
2905 RETURN
2910
```

This subroutine is an outstanding example of grouping features that are not standard. These features are explained to make it possible to rewrite this one subroutine and to run the entire program on a different version of Basic. Grouping unconventional features simplifies program modification.

The code does two important things before it gets down to serious business: it initializes the appropriate variables, and it checks for an empty input file. The program will work even when given an empty file.

```
2915 REM      SUBROUTINE:  POINTER SEARCH
2920 REM         IN:  L$, L()
2925 REM         OUT:  L(), N, W, P1, P2, P3, P4, P5, P6, N2, S$, O$
2930
2935 REM      LINE POINTERS
2940 REM          P1,P2...BEGINNING AND END OF LINE NUMBER.
2945 REM          P3,P4...BEGINNING AND END OF KEYWORD.
2950 REM          P5......BEGINNING OF REM'S COMMENT
2955 REM          P6......BEGINNING OF ON-LINE COMMENT(APOSTROPHE)
2960 REM      EXAMPLE:
2965 REM      P1  P2 P3P4            P6
2970 REM      1   5  8 10            22
2975 REM      I   I  I I             I
2980 REM      22222 LET X = 179      'SAMPLE LINE
2985
2990 REM      BE SURE THE LAST CHARACTER IS A SPACE.   TRIM ALL EXTRA
2995 REM      TRAILING SPACES (IF THE SECOND-TO-LAST CHARACTER IS
3000 REM      A SPACE, DELETE THE LAST CHARACTER).   SEARCH FOR POINTERS.
3005 REM      IF THE LINE BEGINS WITH AN 'IF' (W = 10),
3010 REM      FIND THE 'THEN' LINE NUMBER REFERENCE, N2.
3015
3020     IF L(L(0)) = A(32) THEN 3035
3025       LET L(0) = L(0) + 1
3030       LET L(L(0)) = A(32)
3035
3040     IF L(L(0)-1) <> A(32) THEN 3060 '*
3045       LET  L(L(0)) = 0
3050       LET L(0) = L(0) -1
3055     GO TO 3040                      '*
3060
```

```
3065        GO SUB 3110                   'LINE NUMBER SEARCH
3070        GO SUB 3250                   'KEYWORD SEARCH
3075        IF W <> 10 THEN 3085
3080         GO SUB 3655                  'FIND THEN NUMBER
3085
3090        GO SUB 3880                   'COMMENT SEARCH
3095
3100 RETURN
3105
```

Comment is distinguished from code. The variables are explained and initialized. Notice that a GO TO loop with one or more IF...THEN's at the head is the Minimal Basic way of saying DO...WHILE. Another form is a FOR-NEXT loop with the IF...THEN's occuring at the top of the body of the loop. In both cases the THEN usually exits to a blank line *below* the bottom of the loop. After the loop in the code is completed, four subroutines are called to do four well-defined tasks.

```
3110 REM      SUBROUTINE:  LINE NUMBER SEARCH
3115 REM        IN:  L()
3120 REM        OUT:  N, P1, P2, I
3125
3130 REM      INITIALIZE A CHARACTER POINTER, I, THAT WILL
3135 REM      KEEP TRACK OF HOW FAR THE LINE, L(), HAS BEEN
3140 REM      SEARCHED.
3145
3150 REM      SET POINTERS P1 AND P2 TO THE FIRST AND LAST DIGITS
3155 REM      OF THE LINE NUMBER, N.  STOP WHEN THE CHARACTER IS
3160 REM      NOT A DIGIT BETWEEN  0 (A(48)) AND  9 (A(57)).
3165
3170        LET I = 1
3175        LET P1 = 1
3180        LET P2 = 0
3185        LET N = 0
3190
3195        IF I >= L(0) THEN 3225          '*
3200          IF L(I) < A(48) THEN 3225
3205           IF L(I) > A(57) THEN 3225
3210            LET N = N*10 + FNN(L(I))
3215             LET I = I + 1
3220        GO TO 3195                      '*
3225
3230        LET P2 = I-1
3235
3240 RETURN
3245
```

```
3250 REM      SUBROUTINE:  KEYWORD SEARCH
3255 REM        IN:  L$, L(), I
3260 REM        OUT:  W, P3, P4, I, S$, O$
3265
3270 REM      FIRST CHECK FOR A BLANK LINE (I = L(0)), THEN
3275 REM      PICK UP POINTERS ON THE KEYWORD AND TYPE IT (W = 0-26).
3280 REM      IF THE KEYWORD IS 'GO' (W = 7) THEN PICK UP THE
3285 REM      NEXT WORD TO DISTINGUISH A 'GO TO' FROM A 'GO SUB'.
3290
3295      LET P3 = 0
3300      LET P4 = 0
3305
3310      GO SUB 4115                      'NEXT CHARACTER
3315      IF I < L(0) THEN 3340
3320       LET P3 = L(0)
3325       GO SUB 3420                     'CHECK AND TYPE KEYWORD
3330       LET P4 = L(0)
3335       GO TO 3410                      'RETURN
3340
3345      LET P3 = I
3350      GO SUB 4050                      'NEXT SPACE
3355      LET P4 = I -1
3360
3365      GO SUB 3420                      'CHECK AND TYPE KEYWORD
3370
3375      IF W <> 7 THEN 3405
3380       GO SUB 4115                     'NEXT CHARACTER
3385       GO SUB 4050                     'NEXT SPACE
3390       LET P4 = I - 1
3395       GO SUB 3420                     'CHECK AND TYPE KEYWORD
3400       GO TO 3410                      'RETURN
3405
3410 RETURN
3415


3420 REM      SUBROUTINE: CHECK AND TYPE KEYWORD
3425 REM        IN:  L$, L(), P3, P4
3430 REM        OUT:  W, S$, O$
3435
3440 REM      CHECK TO SEE IF THE KEYWORD IS A LEGAL MEMBER
3445 REM      (W = 1-26) OF MINIMAL BASIC OR A BLANK LINE (W = 0).
3450
3455 REM      WHEN CHECKING THE KEYWORD, SKIP INTERNAL BLANKS (A(32))
3460 REM      IN THE WORD IN THE LINE L(), FOR EXAMPLE, IN 'GO TO'.
3465
3470 REM      THE LOCATION W(H,0) TELLS HOW LONG THE W() VECTOR WILL BE.
3475 REM      THE W() VECTOR FOR THE KEYWORD "LET" IS:
3480 REM           W(H,0)  W(H,1)  W(H,2)  W(H,3)
3485 REM             3       76      69      84
3490
3495      LET J = 0
3500      LET K = 0
3505      LET W = -1
3510
3515      IF P3 <> L(0) THEN 3530
3520       LET W = 0
3525       GO TO 3645                      'RETURN
3530
```

```
3535        FOR H = 1 TO K9
3540           IF W(H,1) <> L(P3) THEN 3615
3545           LET K = P3 +1
3550           LET J = 2
3555           IF K > P4 THEN 3600            '*
3560              IF L(K) = A(32) THEN 3585
3565                 IF L(K) = W(H,J) THEN 3575
3570                 GO TO 3620               'NEXT H
3575
3580                 LET J = J + 1
3585
3590                 LET K = K + 1
3595           GO TO 3555                     '*
3600
3605           LET W = H
3610           GO TO 3645                     'RETURN
3615
3620        NEXT H
3625        PRINT "KEYWORD IS NOT MINIMAL BASIC"
3630        GO SUB 6730                       'ERROR AND GO
3635        GO TO 3645                        'RETURN
3640
3645 RETURN
3650


3655 REM    SUBROUTINE:  FIND THEN NUMBER
3660 REM     IN:  L$, L(), P4, I
3665 REM     OUT:  N2, I
3670
3675 REM    BUILD UP N2, THE VALUE OF THE LINE NUMBER FOLLOWING THE
3680 REM    THEN (A(84),A(72),A(69),A(78)).  Q COUNTS QUOTATION
3685 REM    MARKS A(34)).  Q/2 <> INT(Q/2) ASKS "IS Q NOT EVEN?"
3690
3695        LET N2 = 0
3700        LET Q = 0
3705
3710        FOR J = P4 TO L(0)
3715           IF L(J) <> A(34) THEN 3725
3720              LET Q = Q + 1
3725
3730           IF Q/2 <> INT(Q/2) THEN 3825
3735           IF L(J) <> A(84) THEN 3825
3740            IF L(J+1) <> A(72) THEN 3825
3745             IF L(J+2) <> A(69) THEN 3825
3750              IF L(J+3) <> A(78) THEN 3825
3755               LET I = J + 3
3760               GO SUB 4050               'NEXT SPACE
3765               GO SUB 4115               'NEXT CHARACTER
3770               IF I > L(0) THEN 3820 '*
3775                  IF L(I) >= A(48) THEN 3785
3780                  GO TO 3850            'OKAY EXIT
3785
3790                  IF L(I) <= A(57) THEN 3800
3795                  GO TO 3850            'OKAY EXIT
3800
3805                  LET N2 = N2*10 +  FNN(L(I))
3810                  LET I = I + 1
3815               GO TO 3770               '*
3820
3825
3830        NEXT J
3835        PRINT "PROGRAM STOPPED:  NO 'THEN' AFTER THE 'IF'. STOPPED AT:"
3840        GO SUB 6820                       'ERROR AND STOP
3845
```

```
3850 REM      OKAY EXIT
3855     LET I = I + 1
3860     GO TO 3870                              'RETURN
3865
3870 RETURN
3875
```

LINE NUMBER SEARCH shows a GO TO loop with IF...THEN's that make it a DO...WHILE. KEYWORD SEARCH, FIND THEN NUMBER, and COMMENT SEARCH all use subroutines to do frequently repeated tasks such as finding the next space or the next character that is not a space. KEYWORD SEARCH also calls CHECK AND TYPE KEYWORD to get a reading on the current line's keyword.

This subroutine is a safety feature. What comes out is the error flag, S$. When an error occurs, this routine will print an error message to the terminal before it passes the faulty line to ERROR AND GO which prints it out to the terminal and then passes S$ back to the main routine which skips to PRINT THE LINE to print the line in the output file. This division of labor binds the error message to the error trap in the code, centralizes output of the line to the terminal and centralizes output of the line to the file.

```
3880 REM      SUBROUTINE:  COMMENT SEARCH
3885 REM       IN:  L(), W, I
3890 REM      OUT:  P5, P6
3895
3900 REM      REM (W = 19) COMMENT POINTER, P5, OR
3905 REM      CODE WITH AN ON-LINE COMMENT POINTER, P6.
3910 REM      Q COUNTS QUOTATION MARKS (A(34)).
3915 REM      Q/2 <> INT(Q/2) ASKS "IS Q NOT EVEN?"
3920
3925     LET P5 = L(0)
3930     LET P6 = L(0)
3935     LET Q = 0
3940
3945     IF W <> 19 THEN 3980
3950     GO SUB 4115                            'NEXT CHARACTER
3955     LET P5 = I
3960     IF L(P5) <> A9 THEN 3970
3965      LET P6 = P5
3970
3975     GO TO 4040                             'RETURN
3980
3985     FOR J = I TO L(0)
3990        IF L(J) <> A(34) THEN 4000
3995         LET Q = Q + 1
4000
4005        IF Q/2 <> INT(Q/2) THEN 4025
4010         IF L(J) <> A9 THEN 4025
4015          LET P6 = J
4020          GO TO 4040                        'RETURN
4025
4030     NEXT J
4035
4040 RETURN
4045
```

FIND THEN NUMBER is a solid example of how style reveals structure at a glance. When the proper characters are found, the inner loop, IF I >, goes to work and quits when there are no more numbers. Otherwise, an error is detected and noted.

The variable Q is initialized in FIND THEN NUMBER for use right there. Because it does not appear in the OUT list the reader knows it is not intended for wider use. When Q reappears in COMMENT SEARCH, it is again for local use.

```
4050 REM      SUBROUTINE:  NEXT SPACE
4055 REM        IN:  L(), I
4060 REM        OUT:  I
4065
4070 REM      FIND I, THE POSITION OF THE NEXT SPACE.
4075
4080       IF I >= L(0) THEN 4100            '*
4085          IF L(I) = A(32) THEN 4100
4090          LET I = I + 1
4095       GO TO 4080                        '*
4100
4105 RETURN                                  —
4110
4115 REM      SUBROUTINE:  NEXT CHARACTER
4120 REM        IN:  L(), I
4125 REM        OUT:  I
4130
4135 REM      FIND I, THE POSITION OF THE NEXT CHARACTER NOT A SPACE.
4140
4145       IF I >= L(0) THEN 4165            '*
4150          IF L(I) <> A (32) THEN 4165
4155          LET I = I + 1
4160       GO TO 4145                        '*
4165
4170 RETURN
4175
```

Each of these two subroutines performs a frequently repeated task. Each is small but nonetheless useful. Because the code is collected into a subroutine, it only needs to be written, practiced, and debugged once. After it is correct, it may be conveniently invoked with a GO SUB whenever it is needed.

```
4180 REM     SUBROUTINE:  TYPE THE LINE
4185 REM       IN:  L(), N, W, P5, P6, C2, R()
4190 REM       OUT:  T, T$
4195
4200 REM     TYPE THE LINE AS A NUMBER, T, AND AS A NAME, T$.
4205 REM     T AND T$ WORK AS A PAIR. IF ONE IS ALTERED, THE OTHER
4210 REM     SHOULD BE ALTERED.
4215
4220     LET T = 15
4225     LET T$ = "OTHER"
4230
4235     GO SUB 4265                        'TYPE BY KEYWORD
4240     GO SUB 4505                        'TYPE BY ASTERISK
4245     GO SUB 4610                        'TYPE BY THEN REFERENCE
4250
4255 RETURN
4260
```

Lines may be typed by their keyword, by an apostrophe asterisk ('*), or by being a line referenced by a previous IF...THEN. TYPE THE LINE calls a subroutine to perform each task.

```
4265 REM     SUBROUTINE:  TYPE BY KEYWORD
4270 REM       IN:  L(), W, P5, P6
4275 REM       OUT:  T, T$
4280
4285 REM     FIND LINE TYPES 1-5 AND 8-10 FROM KEYWORDS.
4290
4295     IF W <> 0 THEN 4315
4300     LET T = 1
4305     LET T$ = "BLANK"
4310     GO TO 4495                        'RETURN
4315
4320     IF W <> 19 THEN 4390
4325      IF P5 <> L(0) THEN 4345
4330      LET T = 2
4335      LET T$ = "REM BLANK"
4340      GO TO  4495                      'RETURN
4345
4350      IF L(P6) <> A9 THEN  4370
4355      LET T = 3
4360      LET T$ = "REM ON-LINE"
4365      GO TO 4495                       'RETURN
4370
4375      LET T = 4
4380      LET T$ = "REM"
4385      GO TO 4495                       'RETURN
4390
4395     IF W <> 21 THEN 4415
4400     LET T = 5
4405     LET T$ = "RETURN"
4410     GO TO 4495                        'RETURN
4415
4420     IF W <> 6 THEN 4440
4425     LET T = 8
4430     LET T$ = "FOR"
4435     GO TO 4495                        'RETURN
4440
```

```
4445        IF W <> 13 THEN 4465
4450         LET T = 9
4455         LET T$ = "NEXT"
4460         GO TO 4495                        'RETURN
4465
4470        IF W <> 10 THEN 4490
4475         LET T = 10
4480         LET T$ = "IF...THEN"
4485         GO TO 4495                        ' RETURN
4490
4495 RETURN
4500


4505 REM     SUBROUTINE:  TYPE BY ASTERISK
4510 REM      IN:  L(), W, P6
4515 REM      OUT:  T, T$
4520
4525 REM     CHECK TO SEE IF THE LINE BEGINS OR ENDS A GO TO LOOP
4530 REM     BY CHECKING FOR AN APOSTROPHE-ASTERISK ('*),
4535 REM     (A9, A(42)).  W = 9 FOR A 'GO TO'.
4540
4545        IF L(P6) <> A9 THEN 4595
4550         IF L(P6+1) <> A(42) THEN 4595
4555          IF W <> 9 THEN 4575
4560           LET T = 6
4565           LET T$ = "'* GOTO"
4570           GO TO 4600                      'RETURN
4575                .
4580           LET T = 7
4585           LET T$ = "'* TOP"
4590           GO TO 4600                      'RETURN
4595
4600 RETURN
4605
```

```
4610 REM      SUBROUTINE: TYPE BY THEN REFERENCE
4615 REM        IN:  T$, C2, R(), N
4620 REM        OUT:  T, T$
4625
4630 REM      CHECK TO SEE IF THE CURRENT LINE NUMBER, N, IS
4635 REM      REFERRED TO BY A PREVIOUS 'THEN', AND IF IT IS,
4640 REM      REVISE THE LINE'S TYPE.
4645 REM      R() IS THE STACK OF LINE NUMBERS REFERENCED BY
4650 REM      'THEN'S.  C2 IS THE NUMBER OF THE TOP ITEM IN THE STACK.
4655
4660      IF R(C2) <> N THEN 4770
4665       IF T$ <> "BLANK" THEN 4685
4670        LET T = 11
4675        LET T$ = "THEN BLANK"
4680        GO TO 4775                      'RETURN
4685
4690       IF T$ <> "REM BLANK" THEN 4710
4695        LET T = 12
4700        LET T$ = "THEN REM BLANK"
4705        GO TO 4775                      'RETURN
4710
4715       IF T$ <> "REM ON-LINE" THEN 4735
4720        LET T = 13
4725        LET T$ = "THEN REM O-L"
4730        GO TO 4775                      'RETURN
4735
4740       LET T = 14
4745       LET T$ = "THEN STUFF"
4750       PRINT "STYLE FAULT:   THEN LINE IS NOT BLANK."
4755       PRINT L$
4760       PRINT
4765       GO TO 4775                       'RETURN
4770
4775 RETURN
4780
```

The style fault in the THEN REFERENCE block is the least serious error detected by the program. The code merely notes it presence and continues.

After the line is typed, the real work begins. The proper indentation must be applied to the line.

```
4785 REM      SUBROUTINE:  INDENT AND ERROR CHECK
4790 REM        IN: L$, L(), I1, I2, T, C1, S(), C2, R(), N, N2
4795 REM        OUT:  I1, C1, S(), C2, R()
4800
4805 REM      THIS SUBROUTINE LOOKS AT LINES OF TYPE 6 THROUGH 13
4810 REM      AND ADJUSTS THE FLOATING INDENTATION INDEX, I1.
4815
4820 REM      THE ROUTINE USES TWO STACKS:  AN INDENT STACK,S(C1,J),
4825 REM      AND A THEN REFERENCE STACK R(C2).  ASSOCIATED
4830 REM      WITH EACH STACK IS A COUNTER , C1 FOR S() AND C2 FOR R().
4835 REM      EACH COUNTER KEEPS TRACK OF THE CURRENT LAST
4840 REM      ENTRY OF THE STACK.
4845
4850 REM      WHEN SOMETHING IS ADDED, THE STACK IS "PUSHED", WHEN
4855 REM      SOMETHING IS REMOVED THE STACK IS "POPPED."
```

```
4860 REM     VARIABLES:
4865 REM          I1........THE INDENTATION FOR THE LINE
4870 REM          C1.......CURRENT ROW OF STACK ONE
4875 REM          S(C1,1)..THE KIND OF LINE (T) CAUSING THE INDENT
4880 REM          S(C1,2)..THE THEN LINE NUMBER (N2) OF THE LINE
4885 REM          C2.......CURRENT ROW OF STACK TWO.
4890 REM          R(C2)....THE THEN LINE NUMBER REFERENCE STACK
4895 REM          N2.......THE THEN LINE NUMBER
4900 REM          T1.......THE CORRECT LOOP 'TOP' TYPE (LIKE T)
4905
4910      LET T1 = 0
4915
4920      ON T-5 GO TO 4930,4970,4970,5000,5040,5145,5145,5145,5145
4925
4930 REM     THE '*GOTO
4935 REM     T1 = 7 MEANS PROPER TOP IS *TOP.
4940
4945      LET T1 = 7
4950
4955      GO SUB 5225                       'LOOP BOTTOM
4960      GO TO 5215                        'RETURN
4965
4970 REM     A LOOP TOP---FOR OR '*TOP
4975
4980      GOSUB 5345                        'PUSH INDENT STACK
4985      LET I1 = I1 + I8
4990      GO TO 5215                        'RETURN
4995
5000 REM     NEXT
5005 REM     T1 = 8 MEANS PROPER TOP IS FOR.
5010
5015      LET T1 = 8
5020
5025      GO SUB 5225                       'LOOP BOTTOM
5030      GO TO 5215                        'RETURN
5035
5040 REM     IF...THEN
5045
5050      IF N2 > N THEN 5070
5055       PRINT "PROGRAM STOPPED:  IF...THEN DOES NOT "
5060       PRINT "POINT DOWN THE PAGE.  STOPPED AT:"
5065       GO SUB 6820                      'ERROR AND STOP
5070
5075      IF N > R(C2) THEN 5090
5080       IF N2 > R(C2) THEN 5090
5085       GO TO 5115                       'THEN BOTTOM
5090
5095      PRINT "PROGRAM STOPPED:  IF...THEN IS NOT NESTED."
5100      PRINT "LAST THEN LINE NUMBER REFERENCE WAS "; R(C2)
5105      PRINT "STOPPED AT:"
5110      GO SUB 6820                       'ERROR AND STOP
5115
5120      GO SUB 5345                       'PUSH INDENT STACK
5125      LET I1 = I1 + I9
5130      GO SUB 5495                       'PUSH THEN REFERENCE STACK
5135      GO TO 5215                        'RETURN
5140
```

```
5145 REM      THEN REFERENCE
5150
5155      IF S(C1,2) <> N THEN 5175      '*
5160         LET I1 = I1 - I9
5165            GO SUB 5420                 'POP INDENT STACK
5170      GO TO 5155                      '*
5175
5180      IF R(C2) <> N THEN 5195        '*
5185         GO SUB 5570                  'POP THEN REFERENCE STACK
5190      GO TO 5180                      '*
5195
5200      GO TO 5215                      'RETURN
5205
5210
5215 RETURN
5220
```

This subroutine exceeds one page, but its excuse is a good one. The subroutine is really a CASE statement with several self-contained blocks of program, so the reader will not have trouble.

```
5225 REM      SUBROUTINE:  LOOP BOTTOM
5230 REM        IN:  L$, I1, T1, C1, S()
5235 REM        OUT:  I1, C1, S()
5240
5245 REM      POP ANY IF...THEN (T = 10) INDENTATION AND THEN POP THE
5250 REM      INDENTATION FOR THE CORRECT LOOP TOP (T1).
5255
5260      IF S(C1,1) <> 10 THEN 5280     '*
5265         LET I1 = I1 - I9
5270            GO SUB 5420                 'POP INDENT STACK
5275      GO TO 5260                      '*
5280
5285      IF S(C1,1) <> T1 THEN 5305
5290         LET I1 = I1 -I8
5295         GO SUB 5420                  'POP INDENT STACK
5300         GO TO 5335                   'RETURN
5305
5310      PRINT "PROGRAM STOPPED:  LOOPS ARE NOT NESTED.  CURRENT "
5315      PRINT "'BOTTOM' DOES NOT AGREE WITH LAST 'TOP'"
5320      PRINT "STOPPED AT:"
5325      GO SUB 6820                      'ERROR AND STOP
5330
5335 RETURN
5340
5345 REM      SUBROUTINE: PUSH INDENT STACK
5350 REM        IN:  L$, T, C1, S(), N2
5355 REM        OUT:  C1, S()
5360
5365      LET C1 = C1 + 1
5370      IF C1 <= D9 THEN 5390
5375       PRINT "PROGRAM STOPPED: NUMBER OF INDENTS EXCEEDED "; D9
5380       PRINT  "STOPPED AT:"
5385         GO SUB 6820                  'ERROR AND STOP
5390
5395      LET S(C1,1) = T
5400      LET S(C1,2) = N2
5405
5410 RETURN
5415
```

```
5420 REM     SUBROUTINE:  POP INDENT STACK
5425 REM       IN:  L$, C1, S()
5430 REM      OUT:  C1, S()
5435
5440     LET S(C1,1) = 0
5445     LET S(C1,2) = 0
5450
5455     LET C1 = C1 - 1
5460     IF C1 >=0 THEN 5480
5465      PRINT "PROGRAM STOPPED:   'OUTDENTS' EXCEEDED 'INDENTS'."
5470      PRINT "STOPPED AT:"
5475      GO SUB 6820                          'ERROR AND STOP
5480
5485 RETURN
5490
```

The LOOP BOTTOM subroutine performs a single function as do the pair, PUSH INDENT STACK and POP INDENT STACK. Both PUSH and POP check for serious errors. Such checking helps keep the program robust.

```
5495 REM     SUBROUTINE:  PUSH THEN REFERENCE STACK
5500 REM       IN:  L$, C2, R(),N2
5505 REM      OUT:  C2, R()
5510
5515     LET C2 = C2 +1
5520     IF C2 <= D9 THEN 5540
5525      PRINT "PROGRAM STOPPED: NESTED IF...THEN'S EXCEED "; D9
5530      PRINT "STOPPED AT:"
5535      GO SUB 6820                          'ERROR AND STOP
5540
5545     LET R(C2) = N2
5550
5555
5560 RETURN
5565

5570 REM     SUBROUTINE:  POP THEN REFERENCE STACK
5575 REM       IN:  L$, C2, R()
5580 REM      OUT:  C2, R()
5585
5590     LET R(C2) = 0
5595
5600     LET C2 = C2 -1
5605     IF C2 >= 0 THEN 5625
5610      PRINT "PROGRAM STOPPED:  MORE 'THEN' LINES THAN 'IF' LINES."
5615      PRINT "STOPPED AT:"
5620      GO SUB 6820                          'ERROR AND STOP
5625
5630 RETURN
5635
```

Here are two cautious workhorses, each of which performs a simple task.

The last big subroutine exhibits several familiar features. It prepares different kinds of lines by calling the appropriate subroutines.

```
5640 REM      SUBROUTINE:  PREPARE OUTPUT LINE
5645 REM        IN:  L$, L(), I1, I2, P1, P2, P3, P4, P5, P6, T, T$
5650 REM        OUT:  S$, O$
5655
5660 REM      INITIALIZE THE TEMPORARY STORAGE, I3, FOR THE INDENT
5665 REM      VARIBLE, I1.  PREPARE THE LINE FOR PRINTING
5670 REM      BY APPROPRIATE TYPE, T.
5675
5680      LET I3 = 0
5685
5690      IF T > 7 THEN 5700
5695       ON T GO TO 5710,5710,5745,5745,5745,5925,5870
5700       ON T-7 GO TO 5870,5925,5870,5710,5710,5745,5925,5925
5705
5710 REM      BLANKS AND REM BLANKS
5715
5716      LET I3 = I1
5717      LET I1 = 1
5720      GO SUB 5965                        'BLANK CHECK AND CHANGE
5725      GO SUB 6145                        'PREPARE THROUGH KEYWORD
5730      GO SUB 6590                        'CHECK LINE LENGTH
5732      LET I1 = I3
5735      GO TO 5955                         'RETURN
5740
5745 REM      REM ON-LINE, RETURN, AND REGULAR REM
5750
5755 REM      WHATEVER THE CURRENT I1, ONLY INDENT 1 SPACE.  CHECK
5760 REM      FOR A REM ON-LINE OR A RETURN.  BE SURE THE REM COMMENT
5765 REM      IS TABBED AT LEAST R9 SPACES.
5770
5775      LET I3 = I1
5780      LET I1 = 1
5785      GO SUB 6145                        'PREPARE THROUGH KEYWORD
5790      LET I1 = I3
5795
5800      IF T$ <> "REM ON-LINE" THEN 5820
5805       GO SUB 6300                       'PREPARE AFTER KEYWORD
5810       GO SUB 6590                       'CHECK LINE LENGTH
5815       GO TO 5955                        'RETURN
5820
5825      IF T$ <> "RETURN" THEN 5845
5830       GO SUB 6300                       'PREPARE AFTER KEYWORD
5835       GO SUB 6590                       'CHECK LINE LENGTH
5840       GO TO 5955                        'RETURN
5845
5850      GO SUB 6450                        'PREPARE AFTER REM
5855      GO SUB 6590                        'CHECK LINE LENGTH
5860      GO TO 5955                         'RETURN
5865
5870 REM      INDENT TOP LINE--FOR, IF...THEN, OR '*TOP
5875
5880      LET I3 = I1
5885      LET I1 = I2
5890      GO SUB 6145                        'PREPARE THROUGH KEYWORD
5895      LET I1 = I3
5900
5905      GO SUB 6300                        'PREPARE AFTER KEYWORD
5910      GO SUB 6590                        'CHECK LINE LENGTH
5915      GO TO 5955                         'RETURN
5920
5925 REM      OTHER CODE LINES
5930
5935      GO SUB 6145                        'PREPARE THROUGH KEYWORD
5940      GO SUB 6300                        'PREPARE AFTER KEYWORD
5945      GO SUB 6590                        'CHECK LINE LENGTH
5950
5955 RETURN
5960
```

Here are four subroutines that prepare lines for printing. Each is a neat, clean function.

```
5965 REM       SUBROUTINE:  BLANK CHECK AND CHANGE
5970 REM         IN:  L(), P1, P2, P3, P4, T
5975 REM         OUT:  L(), P3, P4
5980
5985 REM       IF LINE IS BLANK AND YOU WANT IT BLANK (B9=1), SKIP IT.
5990 REM       IF LINE IS REM BLANK AND YOU WANT IT (B9=0), SKIP IT.
5995 REM       OTHERWISE CHANGE THE LINE TO THE OTHER FORM.
6000
6005       IF T > 7 THEN 6015
6010         ON T GO TO 6025,6090,6135,6135,6135,6135,6135
6015         ON T-7 GO TO 6135,6135,6135,6025,6090,6135,6135,6135
6020
6025 REM     BLANKS
6030       IF B9 = 1 THEN 6075
6035         LET L(P2+1) = A(32)
6040         LET L(P2+2) = A(82)
6045         LET L(P2+3) = A(69)
6050         LET L(P2+4) = A(77)
6055         LET L(P2+5) = A(32)
6060         LET L(0) = P2 + 5
6065         LET P3 = P2 + 2
6070         LET P4 = P2 + 4
6075
6080       GO TO 6135                     'RETURN
6085
6090 REM     REM BLANKS
6095       IF B9 = 0 THEN 6120
6100         LET L(P2+1) = A(32)
6105         LET L(0) = P2 + 1
6110         LET P3 = L(0)
6115         LET P4 = L(0)
6120
6125       GO TO 6135                     'RETURN
6130
6135 RETURN
6140
```

```
6145 REM      SUBROUTINE:  PREPARE THROUGH KEYWORD
6150 REM        IN:  L(), I1, P1, P2, P3, P4
6155 REM        OUT:  I, O()
6160
6165 REM        INITIALIZE THE OUTPUT VECTOR, O(),  AND THE
6170 REM        OUTPUT CHARACTER POINTER, I.
6175 REM        PREPARE THE LINE NUMBER, P1-P2, THE
6180 REM        INDENTATION, I1, AND THE KEYWORD, P3-P4.
6185
6190      FOR I = 1 TO O9
6195         LET O(I) = 0
6200      NEXT I
6205      LET I = 1
6210
6215      FOR J = P1 TO P2
6220         LET O(I) = L(J)
6225         LET I = I + 1
6230      NEXT J
6235
6240      FOR J = 1 TO I1
6245         LET O(I) = A(32)
6250         LET I = I + 1
6255      NEXT J
6260
6265      FOR J = P3 TO P4
6270         LET O(I) = L(J)
6275         LET I = I + 1
6280      NEXT J
6285
6290 RETURN
6295


6300 REM      SUBROUTINE:  PREPARE AFTER KEYWORD
6305 REM        IN:  L(), I, P4, P6, O()
6310 REM        OUT:  I, O()
6315
6320 REM      PREPARE THE LINE OVER TO AN ON-LINE COMMENT, P6.
6325 REM      FILL WITH SPACES, A(32), UNTIL THE COMMENT IS IN
6330 REM      POSITION C9, AND CONCLUDE THE LINE.
6335
6340
6345      FOR J = P4+1 TO P6-1
6350         LET O(I) = L(J)
6355         LET I = I + 1
6360      NEXT J
6365
6370      IF P6 <> L(0) THEN 6385
6375       LET O(I) = L(P6)
6380       GO TO 6440                        'RETURN
6385
6390      IF I >= C9 THEN 6410               '*
6395         LET O(I) = A(32)
6400         LET I = I + 1
6405      GO TO 6390                         '*
6410
6415      FOR J = P6 TO L(0)
6420         LET O(I) = L(J)
6425         LET I = I + 1
6430      NEXT J
6435
6440 RETURN
6445
```

```
6450 REM      SUBROUTINE:  PREPARE AFTER REM
6455 REM       IN:  L(),  P4, P5, I, O()
6460 REM      OUT:  I, O()
6465
6470 REM      BE SURE THAT AT LEAST R9 SPACES FOLLOW
6475 REM      THE REM.  THEN PREPARE THE REST OF THE LINE.
6480
6485      FOR J = P4+1 TO P5-1
6490         LET O(I) = L(J)
6495         LET I = I + 1
6500      NEXT J
6505
6510      IF P5 <> L(0) THEN 6525
6515       LET O(I) = L(P5)
6520       GO TO 6580                    'RETURN
6525
6530      IF I > P4+R9 THEN 6550         '*
6535         LET O(I) = A(32)
6540         LET I = I + 1
6545      GO TO 6530                     '*
6550
6555      FOR J = P5 TO L(0)
6560         LET O(I) = L(J)
6565         LET I = I + 1
6570      NEXT J
6575
6580 RETURN
6585
```

A final check to be sure that the output is of acceptable length. This subroutine also contains some unconventional features. Because the features are isolated, the program is easy to modify for use on another system.

```
6590 REM      SUBROUTINE:  CHECK LINE LENGTH
6595 REM       IN:  L$, I, O()
6600 REM      OUT:  S$, O$
6605
6610      LET O$ = " "
6615      LET E$ = " "
6620      FOR J = 1 TO E9
6625         LET E(J) = 0
6630      NEXT J
6635
6640      LET O(0) = I
6645      IF O(0)-1 <= W9 THEN 6705
6650       PRINT "STYLED LINE LONGER THAN"; W9 ;"CHARACTERS. EXCESS IS"
6655      LET E(0) = O(0) - W9
6660      FOR J = W9+1 TO O(0)
6665         LET E(J-W9) = O(J)
6670      NEXT J
6675
6680      CHANGE E TO E$               'NOT MINIMAL BASIC ***
6685      PRINT E$
6690
6695      GO SUB 6730                  'ERROR AND GO
6700      GO TO 6720                   'RETURN
6705
6710      CHANGE O TO O$               'NOT MINIMAL BASIC ***
6715
6720 RETURN
6725
```

Two error routines are each collected around a function. Notice how
ERROR AND GO sets S$ = "SKIP LINE" and S$ makes an orderly return up
through the program until it gets to the main loop of the program where the
error is detected and the flow is interrupted.

ERROR AND STOP prints a faulty line and stops.

```
6730 REM      SUBROUTINE:   ERROR AND GO
6735 REM        IN:   L$
6740 REM        OUT:   S$, O$
6745
6750 REM      PRINTS THE CURRENT LINE TO THE TERMINAL, SETS THE
6755 REM      SKIP FLAG, S$, AND PASSES THE OUTPUT LINE, O$, BACK
6760 REM      TO THE MAIN ROUTINE WHICH SKIPS FURTHER WORK AND
6765 REM      PRINTS O$ TO THE OUTPUT FILE.
6770
6775      LET O$ = " "
6780
6785      LET O$ = L$
6790      PRINT O$
6795      PRINT
6800      LET S$ = "SKIP LINE"
6805
6810 RETURN
6815

6820 REM      SUBROUTINE:   ERROR AND STOP
6825 REM        IN:   L$
6830 REM        OUT:
6835
6840      LET O$ = L$
6845      PRINT O$
6850      STOP
6855
6860 RETURN
6865
```

PRINT OUT LINE is a separate subroutine because it is the only place in the
program where a line gets written to the output file. To be sure the output is
completely under control is worth the few extra lines of code needed to create a
separate subroutine.

```
6870 REM      SUBROUTINE: PRINT OUT LINE
6875 REM        IN:   O$
6880 REM        OUT:
6885
6890      PRINT #2: O$                      'NOT MINIMAL BASIC ***
6895
6900 RETURN
6905
6910      END
```

"Begin at the beginning," the King said very gravely, "and
go on till you come to the end: then stop."

LEWIS CARROLL
Alice's Adventures in Wonderland

Bibliography

Preface

American National Standards Institute, *Minimal BASIC*, Publication Number X3.60, 1430 Broadway, New York, NY 10018, 1977.

Shneiderman, B., Mayer, R. , McKay, D., and Heller, P., "Experimental Investigations of the Utility of Detailed Flowcharts in Programming," *Communications of the ACM*, Vol. 20, No. 6, June 1977, pp. 373-381.

Strunk, W., and White, E.B., *The Elements of Style*, 2nd edition, New York: The Macmillian Company, 1972.

Chapter 1

Adams, J.L., *Conceptual Blockbusting; A Pleasurable Guide to Problem Solving*, San Francisco: San Francisco Book Company, Inc., 1976.

Descartes, R., *Rules for the Direction of the Mind*, Chicago: Great Books of them Western World, Vol. 31, Encyclopaedia Britannica, Inc., 1952.

-------------, *Discourse on Method*, Chicago: Great Books of the Western World, Vol. 31, Encyclopaedia Britannica, Inc., 1952.

Knuth, D.E., "Fundamental Algorithms," Vol. 1 of *The Art of Computer Programming*, 2nd edition, Reading, MA: Addison- Wesley Publishing company, 1973.

Polya, G. *How to Solve It*, 2nd edition, Garden City, NY: Doubleday & Company, Inc., 1957.

Wickelgren, W. A., *How to Solve Problems*, San Francisco: W.H. Freeman and Company, 1974.

Chapter 2

Kernighan, B.W., and Plauger, P.J., *The Elements of Programming Style*, New York: McGraw-Hill Book Company, 1974.

Weinberg, G.M., *The Psychology of Computer Programming*, New York: Van Nostrand Reinhold Company, 1971.

Chapter 3

Baker, S., *The Practical Stylist*, 2nd edition, New York: Thomas Y. Crowell Company, 1969.

Fowler, H.W., *Modern English Usage*, 2nd edition revised by Sir Ernest Gowers, New York: Oxford University Press, 1965.

Morris, W., ed., *The American Heritage Dictionary of the English Language*, New York: American Heritage Publishing Co., Inc., 1969.

Chapter 4

Ledgard, H.F., *Programming Proverbs*, Hayden Book Company, Inc., 1975.

Brooks, F.P. ,Jr., *The Mythical Man-Month; Essays on Software Engineering*, Reading MA: Addison-Wesley Publishing Company, 1975.

Chapter 5

Dwyer, T., and Critchfield, M., *BASIC and the Personal Computer*, Reading MA: Addison-Wesley Publishing Company, 1978.

Kemeny, J.G., and Kurtz, T.E., *BASIC Programming*, 2nd edition, New York: John Wiley & Sons, Inc. 1971.

Shell, D.L., "A High-Speed Sorting Procedure," *Communications of the ACM*, Vol. 2, July, 1959, pp. 30-32.

Tukey, J., *Exploratory Data Analysis*, Reading, MA: Addison-Wesley Publishing Company, 1977.

Chapter 6

Dahl, O.-J., Dijkstra, E.W., and Hoare, C.A.R., *Structured Programming*, New York: Academic Press, 1972.

Garland, S.J., *Structured Programming, Graphics and BASIC,* Special Publication 26, Hanover, NH: Kiewit Computation Center, Dartmouth College, 1976.

Kernighan, B.W., and Plauger, P.J., *Software Tools,* Reading MA: Addison-Wesley Publishing Company, 1976.

Stevens, W.P., Meyers, G.J. and Constantine, L.L., "Structured Design," *IBM Systems Journal,* Vol. 13, No. 2, 1974, pp. 115-139.

Waite, S.V.F., and Mather, D.G., eds., *BASIC: Sixth Edition,* Hanover, NH: University Press of New England, 1971.

Yourdan, E., *Techniques of Program Structure and Design,* New York: Prentice-Hall, 1976.

Index